Church
in the
Wildwood

A Novel of Discovery

Church
in the
Wildwood

Catherine Ritch Guess

CRM BOOKS
Publishing Hope for Today's Society
Inspirational Books~CDs~Children's Books

CRM BOOKS, P.O. Box 2124, Hendersonville, NC 28793

Visit our Web site at www.ciridmus.com

The Reality Fiction name and logo are registered trademarks of CRM BOOKS.

Printed in Canada

ISBN: 0-9713534-9-2
LCCN: 2005903100

To

Randy Pace

Who introduced me to
Cedar Mountain

and

Joe *and* Chris Pace

My Burrell and Flora

Books by
Catherine Ritch Guess

Eagles Wings Trilogy
LOVE LIFTED ME
HIGHER GROUND

Shooting Star Series
IN THE BLEAK MIDWINTER
A SONG IN THE AIR

Sandman Series
OLD RUGGED CROSS
LET US BREAK BREAD TOGETHER

IN THE GARDEN

Acknowledgments

To Kelly's Restaurant in Brevard, NC, and to Thelma, Doug, Randy, Regina and Michael Pace (and their families) and "Mrs. B"; and to the Kelly's Gang - Buster and Joan, Charlie and Barbara, Preacher and Pat, Moby and Preacher Ron Nelson - who allowed me to become a part of the action at Kelly's; and to Dot, Diane and Ralph Lee, Jr. who graciously took me into their family

To the members of BlueRidge Baptist Church - Charles Pierson, Minister; Rocky Hills Baptist Church - Alton Taylor, Minister; McGaha Chapel and First United Methodist Church, Brevard, NC - Fred Jordan, Minister

To St. Mark's United Methodist Church, Indialantic, Florida - Nate Steury, Minister and to Milly and Ken Childress, two terrific characters for quite a memorable welcome; and to the Blueberry Muffin Restaurant and Pearl for a novel breakfast

To Raymond and Barbara Baker, the first individuals I met when I visited Cedar Mountain - I will treasure the ornament always!

To Phil and Ellen Yarborough and Mountain Living Realty for the use of their most inspirational cabin; Mary Jane Howard for her recipes; Lucille Dahl, Vera Stinson, Bobby Jones, and ALL of the members of the Transylvania County churches who have provided help, support and information in the research of this book

To White Squirrel Shoppe, Kris' Klassics, Celestial Mountain Music and Transylvania String Band - Rev. Bill Voorhes, Director

To Grammy's and Mac for going beyond the call of duty to help the local author; to Traci and Bonnie of Kelly's for their support

To Ted and the Cedar Mountain Hardware for help whenever needed

To Wayne and Lenoir Bishop and Nira Lowery for allowing me to make mountain music with them

And to all who so graciously gave of their time and wisdom in the research of *Church in the Wildwood*, many thanks!

Catherine Ritch Guess

A Note from the Author

Writers are a vulnerable people. No matter whether their pages are fiction, non-fiction, poetry, drama – any means of the "word" – readers and the public get a glimpse of the authors through those pages. Their inner thoughts, their creative mind, their upbringing . . . some glimpse into their lives.

With *Church in the Wildwood*, you are getting a vivid look into my environment; albeit the story is totally fictional, the people and places that inspired it are very real – they are my friends and neighbors. They are the people who showed me the beauty of Transylvania County through the way they treated those around them. I live between the tops of two mountains, surrounded by God's handiwork of natural waterfalls that are, for the most part, exactly like they were generations ago. Even the characters, who are long dead and gone, of whom I've heard tales are very real to me as I walk these hills and sit atop Pretty Place and Long Rock and hike Pinnacle Mountain.

I have met people all around the globe during my lifetime of travels, but none that were more genuinely down-to-earth and "real" than the characters I've met in Cedar Mountain. So you'll see, as you turn these pages, that where I live and write truly is, as Ralph Lee, Jr. says, "a fairytale land that is real."

Welcome to my side(s) of the mountain.

- - C?

P.S. – And Michael, "Kick the pig!"

Church
in the
Wildwood

Chapter 1

Talitha Slagle took the last few remaining items from her center desk drawer. It seemed strange that in the modern world of the twenty-first century, her journalism job – the one she had so long dreamed about as a child – had amounted to an office no different than the ones she'd seen in the old movies from the sixties when she was a young child. Those same "screen" characters that had aspired her to this career looked precisely like the ones she was now leaving for a new career.

Or should I say, a different form of the same career. A recent change in her situation had provided Talitha with the opportunity to take her childhood dream a step further and become a freelance writer for magazines, specifically with travel and feature articles.

She picked up the last remaining item from her desk, a framed photograph of her grandfather with her as a child. It had been taken on her third birthday with her sitting perched on his lap unwrapping the baby doll he'd given her. The smiles on their faces made it difficult to discern which one of them was having the bigger time with the event.

Talitha yelled over to Calvin Lowe, her long-time co-worker, as she held the photograph toward his direction.

"This is my first memory of my grandfather. He's the man who made this move possible." She turned the frame back toward herself and wiped off the glass with her sleeve. "Everyone told me that I inherited his sandy-blonde hair and green eyes, and that if I'd been a boy, I'd have been the spitting image of him."

"Here, let me see that," requested Calvin. "Sandy-blonde hair and green eyes are not all you inherited from him," he added, giving her an understanding wink.

She dismissed his last comment, not wanting to make a public statement about her current state of affairs. "They say I got his personality, too. He was always very laid-back and enjoyed people. 'But never wasted a minute of nary a day,' my grandmother would say."

Calvin handed the picture back as he listened to her admiring words.

"He was the kindest man I ever met, and I'm not saying that just because I'm prejudiced."

"From the stories you've told me about you two, I'd say he liked you just as much."

"I was very fortunate."

"That could be the understatement of the year. That was quite a small fortune he left you. What you got in that one check is probably more money than I'll see in my lifetime sitting behind this desk!"

"Oh, c'mon. It's not that much," she defended shyly. *Perhaps I shouldn't have told him the actual amount.*

"I'm nothing but happy for you, Tally. If there was ever anyone who deserved this break, it was you."

Again, Talitha felt herself blushing. His kindness made up for the dislike she had for the nickname he'd given her from the day she first walked in this office, straight out of college, and sat across from him. In all the years she'd been here, he had continued to call her that name. And in all the years he'd called her that, she had never grown any more used to it.

She looked at him, appreciating the mature sincerity in his blue eyes, so light that they almost appeared gray. His black hair was not any more gray, nor his head any more bald than it had been on that day seventeen years prior. The man had kept his same weight and she was sure that he was still wearing the same sweater vests that he had that first winter. In his shirt pocket was the same pipe that he'd carried all that time, but that she'd not once seen him smoke.

Calvin had become her dearest friend, and although he had been the one person she had confided in at the time of her divorce, neither of them had ever pushed the issue that they were both "single again." He was a respected co-worker who had taught her the ropes and been an encourager in the "down" times.

Talitha had watched him turn down numerous offers or

promotions simply because he was content writing feature articles and, as he said, "making people look good on the page in this day of all the bad news." He was hands-down the best reporter of the *Monroe Enquirer-Journal* and had been employed there long enough to watch two papers merge into one, going from a three-day-a-week paper to a daily publication.

Now as she sat looking at him, in retrospect, she couldn't help but wonder whether he looked precisely as he had the day he began work for the newspaper. A part of her wanted to go through the archives to see if he'd been there all those years ago when, as a child, she rushed to get the paper for her mother as soon as it was delivered. He was one of those people who never seemed to age.

She focused on getting a final glimpse of the magnetism in his expression that made people trust him. *Maybe why he's done so well as a feature reporter. The people he interviewed probably took one look at him and spilled their lives' stories right on the table.*

It was the same expression that was on his face that first day. *"Welcome to the office, Tally. Glad to have you in my department."* She could still hear those words. Talitha looked squarely into those eyes. *Perhaps it was that same combination of kind words and honest eyes that caused me not to say anything about the nickname then, too.* She'd never admitted to him her strong dislike for that name, and she decided now was no time to rock that boat. It could wander aimlessly out to sea once she was out of the office.

Realizing she was so engrossed in building a lasting memory of him that she'd failed to respond to his comment, she quickly sputtered, "Thanks. I'm not sure why you said that, but I appreciate your opinion." She gave a slight chuckle. "In fact, *your* opinion is one of the few around here that I really care about."

Talitha had much more of a vision than most of the people around her. The fact of the matter was that she'd have probably left years ago if her desk had not butted up to Calvin's - the extent of "that office" to which he'd so graciously welcomed her. He shared her same goals and aspirations, and enjoyed many of the same cultural activities as she did. And over the course of the past seventeen years, he had become a mentor to her. Basically, he had helped her learn to be content with who she was and where she was.

Even so, when the opportunity arose to leave Indian Trail, North Carolina, and go elsewhere, she took advantage of it. She had no idea that her humble grandfather had built such a large sum of money during his career. He had always appeared such an unassuming man, and to look at him, he seemed basically a plain and simple person. For years, she had felt guilty about taking the hundred-dollar bill he gave her each Christmas. In the later years, he had even added several small things that he wrapped and placed under the tree for her.

Talitha loved seeing the pleasure her grandfather received from giving her the presents. Shopping had been a chore that he had abhorred, but as he got older, it became a delightful pleasure for him to get lost in the Christmas crowd to pick out some special little something for her. He would go out nearly every day to pick up an item. She snickered. *The gas to travel to the stores probably cost more than what he actually bought.*

The appreciative granddaughter was unsure whether his new lease on packages under the tree came from his realization that he couldn't take it with him when he went, or his pity for her divorce, leaving her alone in the years that she should have been enjoying children of her own. For whatever reason, Talitha loved her Christmases nowadays as much as she had as a child.

This year, seven weeks before his birthday, a date that fell within days of Christmas, her grandfather died. More than the fact that she would miss him terribly, she realized, as she walked away from the cemetery after his burial, that the thing she was going to miss most was the annual glow on his face. *The one that was so bright that it appeared the lights from the tree reflected from it,* she remembered thinking as she'd opened each year's small pile of holiday gifts.

It should have come as no surprise, but Talitha was more than a bit shocked when an attorney called her one week before what would have been her grandfather's birthday and asked if she could come by his office the following day.

The rest of that day had been spent in anxious anticipation, wondering if her grandfather had left her some small keepsake or memento in his will. She had certainly expected nothing. *But why else would I have gotten a call from his attorney?* Talitha, who as an investigative reporter was always full of questions, repeatedly asked herself all afternoon.

Chapter 2

"Good morning, Miss Slagle," Bernard Tidwell said with a warm smile as he extended his hand. "Thank you for joining me on such short notice."

As Talitha moved toward a chair across from his desk, to which the attorney directed her by the extension of his arm, she mentally rejoiced that she had resumed her maiden name after the divorce. It suddenly seemed like an appropriate tribute to her grandfather to still share that family heritage with him.

She was shocked that Mr. Tidwell joined her by sitting in the other chair that faced his desk rather than staring at her from across the desk. Somehow, she had conjured up a vision of him peering at her through glasses as he looked over the top of the paper from which he would read some statement from a will.

Now he sat looking at her much like Calvin would have done had he been preparing to give her some helpful tidbits on covering a story. "Would you care for a glass of soda or water?"

"No, thank you," Talitha replied in her anxiousness to get back to work to finish a story.

"I'm going to have something. Are you sure? Why don't I have my secretary bring something just in case you change your mind?"

The attorney didn't give the woman in his office a chance to reconsider before he had buzzed his secretary. "Irene, could you bring in a pitcher of water, a bowl of lemon wedges and a couple of glasses of ice."

Talitha sat silent as words came from the other end of the phone line.

"No, I have an assortment of sodas in my refrigerator." Mr. Tidwell hung up the phone and looked directly at the woman seated beside him. "Miss Slagle, your grandfather was a fine man. I represented him for nearly forty years."

A knock at the door indicated that the secretary had arrived with their beverages.

"Yes," Mr. Tidwell called, his lone word giving his secretary the necessary permission to interrupt their conversation.

Irene entered, sat the tray on his desk within their reach, and excused herself.

"Thank you," the executor called behind her. "And Irene, take messages for me until 2:00. I'll be going to lunch following this meeting."

"Yes, sir." She closed the door quietly behind her.

"As I was saying, Ervin Slagle was a loving and considerate person." He reached for one of the glasses and filled it with water. "And he obviously thought a great deal of you."

Talitha smiled. She thought of that picture on her desk when she was sitting on his lap. "He was my very favorite person in the whole world. I knew that if I ever had a problem, Granddaddy was the first person I wanted to talk to. He usually had an answer for everything, and if he didn't, he surely had good ears."

Her smile was reciprocated by the attorney. "I don't know if you were aware of it or not, Talitha . . . I hope you don't mind if I call you by your first name?"

"Oh, no, not at all." *It's a lot better than Tally!*

"Your grandfather had built up a sizeable retirement, enough so that he was able to live off the interest that it generated." The lawyer looked into her face to see there was no change of expression, indicating exactly what he suspected. *She has no idea what's going on here. Glad I had Irene to bring in the water.*

"As you know, you were the apple of your grandfather's eyes. After your divorce, your grandfather made a slight adjustment to his will. Instead of giving all of his inheritance to your father, who has lived a prosperous and comfortable life, he left most of his money to you, with the provision that you would help your father should that ever become necessary. Since both you and your father were only children, this was not a difficult change to make. Your father has been informed of this and he is in total agreement with your grandfather's wishes."

He looked at the still blank stare on her face, but with ears that seemed to perk up with each sentence. Attorney Tidwell reached to his desk and pulled off a file folder. He opened it, revealing its contents as he read from a paper.

"Miss Slagle, Talitha, your grandfather left you an inheritance of $685,000.00. There are a few stipulations, simply provisions that mean that a portion of this money will stay invested as it is so as to provide a supplemental income for you for the rest of your life." He glared up at her. "Your grandfather told me that you had always dreamed of a career as a freelance writer, but had never been able to get ahead financially enough to take that leap.

"Congratulations, Talitha," he announced, handing her a check, "you can now take that leap. And so you won't be too uncomfortable during your transition, here's a check for $215,000.00." Mr. Tidwell moved to stand beside her. "It appears that the gods have smiled on you today." He placed a calming hand on her shoulder. "And your grandfather, too."

The woman in the chair possessed a blank stare, her entire face clearly in a state of shock. "I think I'll have that cola now," Talitha said in a wobbly voice that matched the weakness in her knees. She was grateful that she was sitting with a comfortably padded chair underneath her.

Mr. Tidwell went to the small refrigerator, retrieved a soda and poured it over a glass of ice. "Merry Christmas, Miss Slagle."

"Yes," she acknowledged, from somewhere off in the world that had suddenly engulfed her, "and Happy New Year, too."

Chapter 3

"There's a lot of culture in Brevard, North Carolina. They've got a notable private college so there are quite a few intellectuals and there's a wonderful outdoor theater that brings in a lot of summer stock from the New York area during the summer months. I went to a production of *West Side Story* there several years ago and was most impressed with the set, the performance and the choreography. The actors and actresses were all of superb quality."

Calvin was looking across the table at the map in Talitha's hand. She began to fold it, still wondering where to launch her search for that perfect "writer's retreat."

"Sounds like a good place for starters," she mused aloud. "I think I'll take a serious look into it."

"Let me know what you think after you get in the area. If you like it, I'll know where to find a spare room should I ever get a chance to see another musical at the Brevard Music Center."

"Okay. And if I do settle there, you've got yourself a deal about the room." Talitha laid the money for her lunch on the table.

"Nope," refused Calvin as he picked the money up and handed it back to her. "Couldn't let you get out of town without making sure you had a good last meal."

"Thanks," she accepted with a smile and a wink. "You've been a good teacher. I appreciate all the care and instruction you've given me over the past seventeen years."

"It wasn't anything. I'd have done it for anybody."

And Talitha knew he meant those words. He was the kind of person who would have shared his knowledge with anyone who was willing to accept it. She stood and walked toward the back door of Jud's Restaurant, a Monroe icon, for the last lunch of many she'd shared with her co-worker in this place.

"Hey, Tally," Calvin called behind her, "check out the shops on Main Street. There are some artistically unique spots that I think you'll like. They're the types of places you find off the beaten path. One I particularly remember is called the White Squirrel Shoppe. Be sure to visit it for me."

"Will do," waved Talitha. She could already tell she was going to miss that gentle voice, greeting her with "Good morning, Tally" each day, as she moved as briskly as she could to get out of sight before the tears fell.

Chapter 4

"Where's the best place to eat around here?" asked Talitha as she laid the appreciation gift for Calvin on the counter of the White Squirrel Shoppe.

"What'd you have in mind?" inquired the woman behind the counter.

"A place where the locals go. I want to see the 'real life' of Brevard. Not a tourist hot spot."

"That would be Kelly's," came a voice from the back of the shop. "They're still serving breakfast. Try the pancakes. The best in town."

"It's just down the street on the same side of the road. You can walk there faster than driving," suggested another customer.

"Yeah, but it's a heck of a hike on the way back. We call that 'Jailhouse Hill.' Not nearly as fast getting back as it is getting there," added the customer's husband. "We used to ride our bikes up and down that hill. If you want a real workout, don't go to the gym. Just get out there and walk up and down that hill a few times and you'll be in shape in no time."

"You look like you need to walk up and down it a few times," teased the woman behind the counter, indicating this couple must be regular visitors of the shop. "Work off all those pancakes you've been eating at Kelly's."

Everyone, including Talitha, laughed at the camaraderie between the people and staff in the store. *I could have been this way with Calvin, but certainly no one else in the office. They'd have gotten their feathers too ruffled.*

She paid for her purchase, waited to have it gift-wrapped, then took off down the street toward Kelly's. *Boy, I'll bet the local skateboarders love this place.*

A sign bearing the name of "Kelly's" was within sight. *It must be the place for both locals and tourists,* she judged from all the people lined outside the door. *Or lots of Christmas shoppers. I can't imagine a lunch crowd this big in a town this small.* Talitha glanced at her watch. *But then, it is the official lunch hour. After all those years of trying to beat the lunch crowd in Monroe every day, I should have known better than to come right now.*

I'll ask how long the wait is. I can always wander through the other shops until the crowd lessens. She walked past the waiting guests and in the front door.

"You by yourself?" asked a man behind the counter.

"Yes. How long do you think the wait will be?"

"Not long. The Kelly's Gang just left and we're cleaning those tables right now. I'd say ten minutes max."

"I'll wait," offered Talitha, sure that the hike up Jailhouse Hill to the shops and back would take longer than the ten minutes. She took a seat on one of the outside gliders and enjoyed the nip of the mountains' fresh air while enjoying her favorite pastime – people watching.

In exactly eight minutes, the man from the restaurant stuck his head out the door and called in her direction, "We have a table for you."

"Thanks." Talitha picked Calvin's gift up off the glider and followed him to a booth.

He placed a paper "Hillbilly Expressions" place mat on the thick wooden table in front of her while she slid across the bench. She loved the seat he'd given her for it faced the door and she could continue her favorite pastime. It was also far enough toward the back that she could casually observe all those around her without being noticed. *A perfect spot to see and hear the "real life" of Brevard.*

"What are you having to drink?" he asked.

"Tea, please."

"Sweetened?"

"Yes, please." She gave a friendly smile. "I am still in the South, aren't I?"

He returned the smile. "I had to ask, because we get so many summer people in here that have never seen sweetened tea."

I was right. It is a spot for both locals and tourists. She thought of the restaurant's location in proximity to everything else in the small town. It sat next to the First United Methodist Church and right across the street from Brevard College. *The food would have to be terrible for them not to have a crowd here all the time.* Talitha looked out the front window at the three motorcycles that pulled up to the building. *Not to mention that they're right on the beaten path of everyone who comes through Brevard.*

She glanced over the menu, thinking more that maybe this was the spot she needed to write about for her first travel feature rather than what her food choice for the moment was. A waitress sat a glass of tea on the table, calling Talitha's attention back to the first item of business. *Good, I won't leave this place hungry,* she noted, seeing the large size of the glass. *Restaurants with small glasses usually skimp on the food, too.*

Although her mind told her to order the TAZ salad, her stomach and eyes told her to order the meat loaf.

"We've got Brunswick stew today," the waitress informed someone at a back table.

Brunswick stew? I haven't had that since I used to go to the Unionville barbecue with my grandparents on the first Friday of every November. She closed the menu. *I'd forgotten about that annual tradition with my grandparents. Like everyone else in Union County, they'd go there to meet all the running politicians and share their political views with the other eaters.* Thinking back on the barbecues, that had also included exceptional Brunswick stew, she saw how that yearly fundraiser had been as much a social thing as a culinary event. *Even though it was the best barbecue I ever tasted, ranking right up there with the October barbecues of my street's Stallings United Methodist Church.*

When the waitress came back, Talitha handed her the menu and said, "I'd like the biggest bowl of Brunswick stew that you have."

The host, hearing the comment, laughed and yelled back to the kitchen, "Somebody better grab Buster's bowl. A lady just ordered the biggest bowl of Brunswick stew that we have."

From all corners of the restaurant came trickles of laughter. Talitha had no idea what they were laughing at, but it obviously had something to do with Buster's bowl which, from the reactions of the customers, was quite large and had somewhat of a reputation at Kelly's.

The host came back to Talitha's table and explained. "Buster is one of the Kelly's Gang. They come here for lunch every day. All of them used to come for breakfast, but a couple of them decided they'd like to sleep in since they've retired, so now they all meet here about 10:45. Then they can have either breakfast or lunch, depending on what they want."

Mrs. B, the waitress whose name Talitha had learned by listening to the other customers, brought a bowl and set it down. "Anything else I can get for you?"

"No, if it tastes anywhere near as delicious as it smells, I'm in good shape," Talitha responded with a smile.

Both Mrs. B and the host left her to eat in silence. Having difficulty ignoring the nature of her career, she peered around the restaurant. The wall was covered in prints and photographs, some of them autographed, of old screen stars. Talitha chuckled to herself. The mere act of seeing them brought back memories of Sunday afternoons, perched in her grandfather's lap, while watching the same characters in movies that weren't new even then.

With each bite, she made a game of trying to identify the characters on the wall. She had successfully named them all, except one, when her eyes stopped. Instead of old photos, her eyes became glued to an old walking cane hanging on a wooden support beam in the restaurant. It was hung too high to have been placed there for safekeeping by a customer. The cane had no ornate work or fancy handle. It was a simple wooden stick with a curve at the top for the handle and a white plastic stop on the bottom. It was those simple details that made the cane so noticeable. Or at least the part that Talitha noticed about it.

It looks exactly like Granddaddy's cane, she carefully observed. *Look at all the old scars up the sides. Boy, if that thing could talk, the stories it could tell. I wonder where all it's been. With that many scratches and nicks, it's seen many a mile.* Her eyes continued to examine the cane until she noticed a row of letters carved onto it. *Probably done with a small pocketknife.* "M," she said to herself, anxious to read what it said. "I - C - K," she continued. "E - Y," she finished. "MICKEY."

At least I know the owner's name now. Her eyes darted around the room to find the host. *I'll catch him after he seats the next couple.*

"Excuse me," she called as he passed her. "Could you tell me who this cane belongs to?"

"Oh, that's Mickey's. He died last year and the Gang wanted to keep it here as a lasting memento. Buster said this way they can still eat with him every day. Preacher says it's a reminder that they, too, will one day be feasting at the Big Banquet Table."

Mrs. B passed at that moment. "But I keep telling Preacher they're going to be serving Kelly's food."

"As much as he eats here, they'd better have Kelly's food.

Otherwise, his stomach won't be able to handle the change," joked a woman from a back booth.

"That's Preacher's sister," laughed the host.

Buster and Preacher. Obviously two members of the "Gang." Ah, and Mickey . . . so he was *a family member.* She inwardly grinned. *At least in a manner of speaking,* she surmised as her ears continued to listen to the shared small-town conversation of the rest of the customers. *I should have guessed.*

Talitha continued to observe the varying clientele of the eating establishment. *Which is clearly established,* she noted from the number of parties who walked in and called out to the host and waitress and were greeted in return on a first-name basis. What really amazed her was when the host briskly walked past her and then came back, leading a woman with a walker. He assisted her out the door and to her car, where he helped her get inside, and then took the walker, folded it and placed it behind the passenger seat.

Now that's something I haven't seen at a restaurant in Monroe or Charlotte anytime lately. They're just anxious to take your money, kick you out the door and turn the table for the next guests.

"Surely it isn't that bad."

Talitha turned her head to see another man, who'd taken the host's place of seating people for the moment, and was staring at her in response to her comment. "I'm sorry. Did those words come out loud?"

"Yes," the man snickered.

"Oh, I'm really sorry now. I guess I was so shocked to see that kind of hospitality that I didn't realize I actually said the words."

"It's quite all right," the man laughed. "We get that kind

of reaction from folks passing through here all the time."

"Good! I'd hate to be the only weirdo that's ever visited the place." She laughed, a hint of embarrassment in her voice.

"Naw," chuckled a man seated across the aisle. "We get stranger folks than you all the time. All the tourists seem to flock here."

Talitha smiled at the welcome she was receiving. "Well, you know what they say. 'Birds of a feather flock together.' Maybe they've heard, from all the other tourists, about what a great place this is to visit. That's how I came to be here. Word-of-mouth. A co-worker back home told me about the area."

"Glad you decided to stop in," offered the host who had returned from helping the older woman.

While the three men then briefly exchanged a few words, Talitha stared into the face of the man who had seated her. His brown hair and brown eyes hinted at the natural warmth in his expression, and he exhibited a laugh that soared through the air, allowing the customers to feel his frivolity and love for life. You could tell from his demeanor that he thrived on being a part of this environment and, from his words, that he was a wealth of information in regards to the area and its history and inhabitants. Shortly, the men went back to their previous activities and Talitha went back to her job of people watching.

She was particularly interested in one family who came in and took a spot on the waiting list. There were four young boys, none of them looking to be over eight years old, with a man and woman who were obviously the parents. All four of the children possessed very visible resemblances to both parents, but the one characteristic that really stuck out about the young boys is that they each had a cowlick, and each cowlick was at a different spot on its owner's head.

The host led the family to the table beside Talitha. *Great! Now I can get a birds-eye view of them.* Her intrigue with watching the boys grew as they sat down and began to order their food. She could imagine them running in a big yard, playing Cowboys and Indians and all the other outdoor games of the children of her generation, rather than being stuck on a sofa all day with some hand-held gadget hooked to a TV screen.

"How old are they?" she asked the mother.

Their casual conversation continued until Mrs. B served the family of six.

"Enjoy your visit," offered the mother, turning her attention to making sure her children got the right orders and helping the younger one with cutting his chicken strips.

The family I'd always imagined, thought Talitha, consciously trying not to stare at them as she finished her last few bites of the Brunswick stew.

"Would you like dessert?" asked the original host, propping his arm on the back rail of her booth.

"What do you have?"

"You picked a good day to come. Mama made her famous walnut cake for dessert. She won't share the recipe with anybody, even me. And she only makes it once in a while, when the urge strikes her, for the restaurant. There's only two pieces left in the back."

"Sounds delicious. I'll have to try it."

"Mind if I join you?"

"Not at all," Talitha accepted, finding herself surprisingly grateful for the company of another person.

"So I take it your mom owns the restaurant?" she asked when he returned with two slices of cake and took a seat across from her.

"Yeah. This is a family operation. My mom and dad actually run it and my sister and I help."

"No wonder there's such a distinct family atmosphere. You really are family."

"Uh-huh," he said, taking a big bite of the cake.

"I haven't seen a family-run restaurant in I don't know how long."

"Is that right?" He continued to eat, his response more like a statement than a question.

"This cake is delicious," she said, taking a small bite.

"Why do you think I grabbed the last piece?"

"This stew was great, too. Is the food this good everyday?"

"Yep. Mama is a good cook."

"I've never met a woman in the mountains who wasn't."

"Are you from the mountains?"

"No," admitted Talitha. "But my grandfather was. I'm looking for a place to do some writing and thought the mountains might be a good place to start."

"What kind of writing? Are you an author?"

"No," she smiled. "I wrote for a newspaper, but I'm hoping to write some magazine articles. I thought I might find some good stories around here just waiting to be told."

The man gave a huge burst of laughter. "You wanna hear some good stories? Then you've come to the right place. If there's one thing that we've got more of here than good food, it's good stories."

I'll have to call Calvin and thank him for the tip.

"Hey, Daddy," the man called to the kitchen.

The man who'd taken the place of the host earlier reappeared and sat at the booth. Before long, Talitha was being entertained by both of the men, whom she learned were Randy Heath, and his father, Doug. By the time she left the restaurant, she had four pages full of notes and was on first-name basis with the father and son.

"Come back anytime," invited Doug.

"Oh, I'll definitely be back," she replied, "and probably sooner than later."

"Don't forget to take a drive up toward Cedar Mountain," reminded Randy, again mentioning a neighboring place that he'd suggested she visit while in town.

"Thanks for the tip. I'll be sure to make a trip there."

Talitha got in her car and headed back down the mountain, anxious to put her notes into story form and make a new entry in her journal, a habit she'd begun only yesterday when she finished her notice and said good-bye to the *Monroe Enquirer-Journal*. *There'll be another day for Cedar Mountain. Right now, I've got to start packing up all my things from the duplex. After all, Talitha, your Christmas gift to your grandfather is to begin a search for a new home and a new career.*

Chapter 5

T alitha took a scrutinizing look at the man whom everyone called Moby. He certainly didn't resemble the description of Melville, so there had to be a story behind that name. *Just like all the other stories hidden away in this place.*

It was her second visit to Kelly's in a week and she'd made a point of arriving at mid-morning so she could not only meet, but also watch the antics of, the "Gang." She'd been so enthralled by Randy's character descriptions of its members, during her first visit, that she couldn't resist returning to Brevard to make their acquaintances.

The host readily recognized Talitha the moment she walked through the door. She reviewed his original words in her mind as she followed him to a booth that butted up against the notorious table. "There's Preacher and Pat," he had told her. "Preacher's down at Blue Ridge Baptist Church. Then there's Buster and Joan, and Charlie and Barbara. Buster works at the Pisgah Forest Post Office and Charlie's retired. Moby comes once in a while, but not as much as he used to. Mickey used to come in everyday, but now his cane hangs on the post beside their table for a lasting memory."

Now Talitha was able to put faces with names as she slowly ate her pancakes, listening to them give her a "Cliff's Notes" version of their background as she tried to take in their entire conversation.

"Moby gets into all the football games free," explained Pat, as if this was a statement of great importance, at least where Kelly's Gang was concerned.

"Because you're their mascot from all the years of attendance?" Talitha asked of Moby, after hearing how he'd not missed a game in over twenty-seven years.

"Because he sits on the end and holds the chain," Barbara piped up.

"Holds the chain?" the visitor asked, confused. "Does he have to keep some of the troublemaking students from coming in the gate or something?"

"He measures the distance," explained Preacher.

"You know, the yardage after each play," finished Charlie.

Talitha glanced over at Moby. She loved the fact that he had not opened his mouth the first time. No one seated at the table had allowed him to answer for himself. He was taking a big swig of coffee, unsurprised that everyone had taken care of this conversation for him – like it was expected or that he simply didn't care. The visitor couldn't help but wonder if it had always been this way.

She turned back around thinking how wonderful it was that this group of locals had accepted an outsider, Buster – who was a Yankee from Massachusetts, at that – into their midst. *Maybe I can make a home for myself here and feel welcome after all.*

Preacher got up and walked over to Talitha's booth, while his wife took up Randy's place of leaning on the arm of the booth's bench. "Ya know, Randy's cousin is the preacher of the biggest Baptist church in Indian Trail."

"Whitson Lambert?" Talitha asked in amazement, gulping her food down before choking.

"You know Whitson?" Preacher asked, as astonished as the newcomer at this connection.

"I do know him. I visited that congregation a few times several months ago." She didn't want to admit that she'd gotten out of the habit of going to church years ago, and like many others faced with some type of dilemma, she had only gone back in search of answers after a hurtful divorce. Nor did she admit that although she had intended to go the Sunday after she found out about her grandfather's will, she couldn't pull herself out of bed, or face the people she didn't know.

"He grew up here in Transylvania County. Right in Rocky Hills Baptist Church in Cedar Mountain, straight up 276. His parents still go there," Preacher continued.

"You're kidding?" Talitha found it odd that she was in a place she'd never been before, and already had a connection with the community.

"We've had five preachers to come out of that church," interjected Doug, who walked up and joined the conversation. "One is there now, one works with the NASCAR ministries – he's my nephew in Missouri, one's in South Carolina, another's in Florida, and then there's Whitson."

"And we're kin to all of 'em. We had to go out of the state to keep from marryin' our cousins," Randy confessed.

Talitha laughed aloud, but as she did, she remembered having heard her uncle make that same statement when she was a child. Anytime her family had gotten together and started telling their favorite tales of growing up in the mountains, he'd utter those same words. And she had come from a long line of ministers, as well. She felt right at home. In fact, more at home than she had in her own hometown.

She looked at Doug and Randy, both standing in front of her. Talitha had heard people talk about folks being "the salt of the earth." Now she knew what they meant. These two men were solid, down-to-earth individuals. They had lived life to its fullest in every way possible, and in the first decade of the twenty-first century, their immediate family members all still lived within a five-mile range.

And that five-mile range had turned out five men who were spreading the gospel to people throughout the country. *Not to mention the people who lived in the nearby areas and attended the local churches.*

The tales that Randy and Doug had shared about Cedar Mountain, their home, on that first visit were now being greatly enhanced on this visit. "You ought'a just take a ride on up there,"

Randy encouraged after he found out she'd not yet made the trek.

"How long will it take me to get there?"

"I'd say about 25-30 minutes seeing as you're not used to the road."

As enticingly delightful as an afternoon jaunt to Cedar Mountain sounded, Talitha had promised herself a view of the "real" Cold Mountain in Haywood County, ninety minutes away. This was a perfect winter's day – a sunny dome of bright blue with only a hint of a breeze – that would allow her to see for miles and miles. *A day every travel journalist dreams for.*

Since she had no time clock to punch any longer, Talitha decided to follow her original plan to take a scenic drive through western North Carolina and come back on another day to hear more tales of Cedar Mountain. This four-day excursion had been planned to serve as a scouting expedition to locate a remote mountain area where she could write and simply "be," – "a place that many people worked too hard to ever let go and reach," according to a recent article by Calvin – yet be close enough to culture to feed her soul.

"Feed your soul? My dear Talitha, it isn't culture that you need to feed your soul."

That was odd! Where did those words come from? Talitha, who had made a game of committing to memory the simple sayings of her grandfather and pulling them out whenever she needed his common sense wisdom, was used to hearing the sayings subconsciously serve as reminders to her. But this voice, although the words sounded exactly like something her grandfather might have said, was clearly not her grandfather's voice.

Hmmm . . .

Chapter 6

"Where you been, stranger?" Randy asked with his usual smile, seating Talitha in the booth that backed up to the table of the Gang, as he handed her a menu.

It was January 2nd, a few days since the writer's last visit to Kelly's, but from the reception she received when she walked through the front door, it seemed it had been only yesterday. She had already come to look forward to the relaxed atmosphere of the restaurant and the difference in the way of the life from her flatland background. "I have to make a living, you know. Not like some people who can simply stroll in here every day for either lunch or dinner," she teased.

"And Preacher comes for breakfast and lunch," said Regina, whom Randy introduced as his younger sister. She flashed a big smile and patted the revered minister on the shoulder.

A woman walked through the door and headed toward the table behind Talitha, not even looking to see who was in the place, or what tables were available.

Part of the Gang, Talitha reasoned, not looking up in time to recognize the face.

"Good morning, Joan," welcomed Randy.

"Where's Buster?" came the question from Charlie, who was seated directly behind Talitha.

"He's on his way," Joan answered.

Regina pulled up a chair for Buster for when he came in. Then another frequent guest of the Gang, Preacher Ron, whom Talitha had not yet had the pleasure of meeting, came in and moved two tables together.

"They're getting too big back there. They're having to move tables together," Regina explained to Talitha.

Hearing all the chatter, Preacher Ron welcomed the restaurant's newcomer with, "You never know what's going to happen at this table."

Talitha loved the fact that most of the people who came in the establishment knew each other. Many of them made a point of waving to the Gang the minute they walked in the door.

"That's Preacher's baby brother," Regina said to her, pointing to a man who had entered the restaurant and was moving toward the Gang with his wife.

"Are you sure Buster's coming?" Barbara asked.

"Is that Buster's tea sitting down there?" Pat motioned.

"Watch him, he's going to go back to the kitchen and get his bowl when he gets here," Randy informed Talitha, making sure she got the full effect of the postman's entrance. "Some people have got to where they come in and want a Buster's Bowl of pinto beans or something," he explained, embellishing on the story he'd told her on the first visit. "All the regulars know about Buster's bowl. It's a big deal here."

"He used to always come in on days when we'd have pinto beans, or soup, or something," Regina continued, "and he said the bowls weren't big enough."

"So he went out and bought a big glass bowl for us to fill up," added Mrs. B, passing with an order for another table.

"The first time he walked in here with that thing," Randy laughed, "I told him, 'your fish wants its bowl back.'"

Regina went to retrieve the renowned conversation piece from the kitchen. She returned carrying a huge clear glass dish that could have easily held a goldfish.

Talitha laughed with delight, sure that she couldn't leave this place before seeing Buster in action.

"You'd better get that thing back in the kitchen. I see him walking through the parking lot," warned Charlie.

"What's the soup today?" Preacher asked.

"Chili," answered Mrs. B.

"Is it good?"

"Do you eat here everyday?" Pat asked.

"What's that got to do with the chili?"

"Would you come here everyday if the food wasn't good?"

"I come here to be with Moby and Charlie and Buster, not

to eat."

"I come for the food," belted Buster, coming through the front door. "Eat the chili." He grinned at the Preacher. "And make it two bowls," he called to Mrs. B while making his way to the kitchen.

All the Gangs' eyes darted toward Talitha with an "I told you so" expression as the postman approached the table, his glass bowl full of chili in hand, and sat at his appointed spot. She could tell from the outset that he was not from Transylvania County and was most impressed that this group of hometown folks had so willingly and graciously allowed a Yankee into their midst.

"So how did you wind up in Brevard?" she questioned him.

"I moved here from Massachusetts. Settled here after the Air Force, wanting to find a place for my kids to all go to high school in one place since they'd been moved around during their elementary and middle school years."

There really is hope for me to be accepted here.

Mrs. B came back with a bowl and a handful of crackers. "A bowl of heartburn," she said as she put it on the table in front of Preacher and took off to get her next order.

"I had it Tuesday," Buster stated. "It ought to be ripe by now," he directed, more to Talitha than to the daily lunch crew.

"You have a good holiday?" Preacher threw out the question to everyone seated at the Gang's table after he had said the blessing.

There were nine people seated at the noted table, now all asking each other if they'd had a Happy New Year. *They saw each other only two days ago, they stayed home yesterday to eat greens and peas and hog jowls, and you'd think it's been a month.*

"Had to eat at home yesterday. 'Bout killed me," Buster admitted, never missing a beat with his spoonful of chili.

"Surely Joan's cooking's not that bad," Preacher Ron laughed.

"Huh," sighed Joan. "All he had was a sandwich. I don't even get to cook anymore."

"Are you sorry?" asked Barbara. "I don't miss it one bit."

"Would you like some banana pudding?" Mrs. B asked Talitha, breaking into the conversation.

Talitha was not a lover of the Southern traditional dessert that most people had exchanged for the quick-and-easy variety with whipped topping and instant pudding, but everyone had been so gracious to her that she decided to give it a try. "Sure, why not?"

"Randy had to cook the entire Christmas and New Year's dinners," Regina said, going back to the holiday conversation.

"Yep, cabbage casserole, black walnut cake," Randy began.

"The icing's the key on that one," his sister interrupted.

"What else did you have?" asked Talitha, turning to the holiday chef.

"Leather britches."

"Leather britches?"

"Yeah," he nodded. "You ever heard of them?"

"Heard of them?" Talitha retorted. "My grandmother used to make those. She'd string the beans up around the door of the kitchen and the living room every summer and let them dry. Then she'd can them." Her answer had just earned her a gold stamp from both the regulars and the restaurant owners.

Randy continued to compare old family recipes with the newcomer. "My momma makes the best creamed corn this side of the Mississippi. At least that's what ever'body says, anyway. She says it's not what you put in it, but how you cut it."

"That sounds exactly like my grandmother. She, my aunt and my mom made the best corn I ever put in my mouth. And they said the same thing about it's all in the way you cut it. In fact, my grandma used to think the people where I grew up didn't know how to cut corn."

"You have to have a real sharp knife."

"Yes. That's what my mom said. She had a special knife just for cutting the top off. Then she'd scraped the rest into the pot."

Randy continued to rattle off family favorites and recipes, to which Talitha found herself nodding, for they sounded exactly like the foods on which she was raised.

"Here's your dessert." Regina sat down a bowl of banana pudding that looked exactly like what Talitha's grandmother and mother used to make. The pudding filling was cooked and the meringue topping was browned just like they did it. Talitha could remember standing in a chair beside her mother and licking the spoon and the pot when the pudding had been poured over the vanilla wafers and the bananas. *That was the best part!*

She dug her spoon into the bowl and took out a huge bite. "Tastes exactly like the old Slagle family recipe," she smiled. "It's been a long time since I've tasted banana pudding this good." Talitha listened to the Gang compare notes on their own family recipes as she envisioned her grandmother and mother in a kitchen where the counter was filled with pots, *and spoons to lick*, full of 'fixins' for delectable desserts and fresh vegetables.

"How did you say I get to the town of Cedar Mountain?"

she asked Randy after she'd finished the dessert. Talitha wasn't sure if it was the food, the conversation or the camaraderie, but something had inspired her to make that drive while in the area.

"It's not a town, it's just a community."

"So where exactly does Brevard end and Cedar Mountain start? Is your address Cedar Mountain?"

"Now I live in Sherwood Forest and I have a Brevard address," Regina said.

"Is your son's name Robin?" Talitha asked, jokingly.

"Huh?"

Talitha noticed the confused expression on Regina's face. "Forget it. Bad joke."

"There is a place there called Robin's Barn. People use it for all sorts of meetings and stuff," Regina responded with a smile.

"Everybody used to go there and square dance every Saturday night," Randy said.

"I remember those dances," called Pat. "We went every Saturday for twenty years."

"Twenty years?" came Talitha's astonished response. "Wasn't there anything else to do in Cedar Mountain?" She immediately wished she could reach out and grab her words before they hit earshot. *Too late*, she feared, as she saw the expression on Pat's face.

"What more could you have wanted to do?" the preacher's wife asked. "That was more fun than sitting home and watching Lawrence Welk."

Talitha resisted a great urge to laugh aloud. Somehow the crowd around her did not seem the Lawrence Welk type. "But does Cedar Mountain have a post office? Is that a real place or just a spot in the road named such by the people who live there?"

"Oh, yeah. We have a post office," answered Randy

Regina sat down beside Talitha and began to draw a map on the back of the paper placemat. "It's right beside Mrs. Corn's store . . . the post office, that is."

"That's Mack's Place," explained Randy. "They built a new post office right beside the store. Mrs. Corn's worked there for years. Her husband died and she's run that place by herself for decades."

"What kind of store is it?" Talitha asked, intrigued by the thought of an old country store. The ones that had sat near her house and her grandparents' house during her childhood had been torn down years ago to "modernize" the area.

"Here, let me show you something." Randy went through the door that headed toward the kitchen and reappeared with yesterday's newspaper in his hand. "This is Mrs. Corn."

Talitha saw the large full-color picture of an aged woman with a blue-flowered dress, standing behind a counter. Behind her were shelves of dry goods, and next to her were racks of gum, not like the new flavors, but the kinds she used to see as a child. And beside the gum were small boxes of cough drops. She promptly noticed the orange box made by Luden's that she hated as a child, but that her grandmother would always hand her at church or out shopping every time she would cough. When she finally got old enough to read, she had suggested her grandmother get the cherry flavor in the white box. She noticed from the newspaper photo in the *Transylvania Times* that both kinds were available at Mack's Place.

"How do I get there?"

"You can't. She closed," Regina said, getting up to seat another couple who'd walked in the door.

Like many of the other businesses around here in the wintertime. "When will she reopen?" It was then that Talitha glanced down at the headline to read that the landmark closed with the end of the year. *I'm one day late.* She was crushed. "Don't you think somebody's there? What's she doing with all the stuff?"

"She's probably still there for a couple more days. I think she'd be there," Randy offered.

"Naw, I don't think so," came Barbara's voice. "The article said New Year's Eve was her last day."

"Why don't you just call?" suggested Joan.

Randy reached behind the counter for the phone and began to dial a number.

He didn't even need to look it up. *Does he not only know everybody in the area, but their phone numbers, too?*

Talitha couldn't hear the conversation, but she could tell from his closing words that she would not get the chance to visit Mack's Place.

"She's closed."

"But she lives right behind the store in the white house," Regina quickly threw in. "Maybe you could go see her and she'd let you in the place."

Talitha was touched that everyone she'd met since her walk through this front door was making an effort to not only welcome her, but also help her to learn about the area and find whatever background she wanted. "No, I couldn't possibly do that. I wouldn't want to disturb her. This is probably a very emotional time for her. But I can still drive by and see the store."

Nods of the group behind her and affirmative words from Randy and Regina showed they agreed with her decision. *Besides, it would be an emotional time for me, as well. I'm afraid the loss of Granddaddy and seeing that place closed would be more than I could stand if I tried to talk to her.*

"Maybe I can see in the windows or something," Talitha said in a voice of hope, showing her determination not to be outdone by missing a tradition of Cedar Mountain.

She quickly paid for her meal and set out to find the store. The image of Mrs. Corn sitting there, hands in her lap, staring out the front door of Mack's Place, was all Talitha could envision as she wound her way around curves and hills leading her out of the "cultured" city and toward an unknown fantasy land of the wild.

When Randy said I'd meet myself going and coming up this road, he wasn't kidding, she grinned, taking her time on 276. *No wonder all the motorcyclists come here; this is their kind of road.* The view of mountains all around soon swallowed her up as she drove straight through the middle of them, keeping her eye out for a place that had been not only an icon for over half a century, but a way of life.

Twenty minutes later, she caught a glimpse of it up ahead on the left. "A white building with a sign at the road reading Mack's Place. You can tell where the gas pumps once sat that fueled every mode of vehicle that ever went through Cedar Mountain, no matter whether visitor or local. They were the only source of gas for miles coming out of, or going to, South Carolina." As she pulled into the parking lot and got out of the car, letting it run since she was only going to take a peek, she recalled the last words Randy said as she walked out the door of Kelly's. "Yep, Mrs. Corn's seen ever'body and anybody who's come through these parts over the last fifty years."

Blinds a third of the way up on the windows, and the shade over the front door up, with a sign that read "Closed," was all that greeted Talitha as she inched her way toward the legendary spot in the annuls of Transylvania County history. Her visual image of Mrs. Corn perfectly fit what she saw as she caught a glimpse of the old brass National cash register sitting on a counter laden with gum packets – the old varieties that she'd not seen in years – and the Luden's cough drops she'd recognized from the newspaper, both in the orange and white packages. Old candy, cracker and chip displays sat where they obviously had for generations, and foliage of green plants cascaded from the windowsills to the floor. Everything inside Mack's Place appeared to be the same as it had been fifty years ago except for two things – the sign no longer read "Open" and Mrs. Corn was not in her straight-back cane chair watching out the front door for the passing traffic.

It was only as she began to turn away that she saw her. Mrs. Corn, sitting in her wooden straight-back chair right in the middle of the store, wearing the same blue-flowered dress and a sweater, an afghan covering her hands and lap, and a walker, that had been her support for years, placed conveniently beside the chair. Talitha had to do a double-take to make sure that what she saw through the window of the door was not her imagination trying to recreate a scene from the past. She was not sure that the woman saw her, for she seemed to be lost in her own world, recreating her own scenes from the past.

Talitha slowly moved away from the door and got back in her car, already enchanted by the simple life that greeted her, yet feeling a melancholic chord for a woman who had provided half a century of memories for a lot of folk. There was no question on this day as to whether the car would head back toward Brevard or continue to venture toward Cedar Mountain.

Chapter 7

Talitha's afternoon consisted of an unplanned visit to Cedar Mountain. From the moment she passed the post office and Mack's Place, and the sign on the right that read CEDAR MT, she could sense that there was something magical about Cedar Mountain and its inhabitants. It wasn't an eerie, ghostly kind of feeling. But it was a faraway feel, like some sort of intriguing spirit lurking about in the air, drawing one into its midst. She could hear a soft music playing, probably nothing more than the wind blowing through the branches of the trees. The magic seemed to enter Talitha's being and give her a peace and tranquility. Whatever it was, she wanted to find it. She wanted to be a part of what was going on here. As she slowly winded down Highway 276, taking in the personalized names of each cabin, cottage and house – most of which appeared unoccupied for the remainder of the winter – the writer laughingly wondered at what point she had left the Blue Ridge Mountains, a part of the Appalachians, and entered Camelot.

Within less than ten minutes, she came to a sign announcing the South Carolina line. Talitha had no idea she was that close to the border. When she'd heard the people in Kelly's talking about crossing the line, she took it for granted they meant the spot that divided Brevard from Cedar Mountain.

Or Mount, as the sign says.

After driving back and forth between the state line and Mack's Place, and still finding no sight of Reasonover Road, Talitha finally stopped at Mountain Living Realty – a local real estate office which housed the Cedar Mountain Welcome Center – to ask directions.

"You're only a stone's throw away. Go back toward Brevard, and right past the new fire department building. You have to turn right onto Cascade Lakes Road. Reasonover is to your right immediately after you make the turn. Hope you have time to hunt down Modena Brendle when you get there. She's a ninety-eight-year-old woman who lives hidden way off the road. All the way down at the end of Reasonover Road. She knows all of the stories of Cedar Mountain."

I knew there were stories here! Talitha bragged to herself, her journalism background surfacing. She thanked the woman and rushed to her car, anxious to get to her destination. *And the stories,* she smiled.

"Oh, and if you get to Modena's, be sure to let her know you're there before you get out of the car."

That was a kind warning. Guess she didn't want me to scare the old lady.

The "stone's throw" proved to be an accurate description. Within less than a minute, Talitha had driven from the Welcome Center to Reasonover Road. A hairpin curve welcomed her the moment she made the right turn, an immediate indication that it was time to slow down and "smell the roses" of Cedar Mountain once she hit this point.

Reasonover Road continued to twist and turn, with each curve revealing a cottage or cabin, some which had been there for nearly a century. It was interesting to see that some had remained family getaway homes, some were permanent dwellings, and a few had been transformed into artists' residences. There was even a bed-and-breakfast called The Sassy Goose that sat back off the road. One of the houses was so magnificent that it caused an audible gasp as it came into view on the left side of the road. A large pond served as the front yard of the mansion, and to the back right side of the mass of water sat a cabin that had obviously been there since before the paved road.

The road, which Talitha had expected to be a short mountain road, went on for what seemed several miles, with each mile taking her into a more remote setting. She passed two old cars that collectors would have dearly loved to get their hands on - one of which had a tree growing out of where the hood should have been. All she could think about was the cane from Kelly's and ponder as to whether it had seen any of these back roads and paths, and if so, what tales it could tell.

Then, when it seemed she was leaving civilization as she spotted a sign that indicated the pavement ended ahead, she peaked a knoll, and there sat the most picturesque little country church building Talitha had ever seen. It was a small, white wooden-framed building, with three stained glass windows on the side, and a covered picnic shelter in the back. There was a short ramp leading up to the front door and a little room at the back of the sanctuary, which appeared to have been added after the original construction, with a concrete block for the step.

This has to be Preacher's church. She read the sign. *Yes, Blue Ridge Baptist Church.* The sight of it reminded Talitha of a hymn, *Church in the Wildwood,* that her grandmother played and sang for her as a child. A hymn loved so much by her grandparents that she had never outgrown the fond memories it brought. A hymn she had loved so much as a child that it was the first one she learned to play in piano lessons. *And a hymn they loved so much that it was sung at both of their funerals.*

She refused to allow the last thought to dampen her spirit that was heightened by the atmosphere of her surroundings. *I can't let this opportunity pass me by.*

Seeing a truck in the parking lot, Talitha opted to take a chance on finding someone inside the building. She parked the car in the small parking lot and walked up the ramp, but stopped in place when she came to the front door. There, before her eyes, was a sight she'd never seen on a Baptist Church – *a red door.*

There must also be a story behind this door. She slowly inched it open, anxious to find the story. "Hello," she called out, pausing to see if she got a response.

No response came, so she pushed the door open a little more to disclose a small room of natural-colored wood lining the walls with wooden pews to match. There was a charm that permeated the air, evoking all the senses, inside the sanctuary, but the thing that caught Talitha's eyes was the Christmas tree that stood on the altar.

It was a live tree, not very tall, covered in ornaments that were all different. *Obviously each brought in by a different member,* she reasoned, noting that each ornament appeared to hold special meaning, many of them handmade with either stitching or photos personalizing them. She went from one branch of the tree to another, each one laden with an ornament, until she came to the smallest ornament on the tree. The smallest, yet the one that screamed at Talitha, drawing her hand to reach out and remove it from the tree.

Time seemed to stand still as she took a seat on the step of the altar, right beside where the ornament had hung, and stared at it. For what the woman saw was not merely a molded rubber shape, but a vision of herself as a young child, seated on a piano bench in front of an old upright piano, one hand on the keys and the other clutching her favorite doll. She became so thoroughly engrossed in the small ornament, that was an exact replica of a favorite scene from her childhood, that she did not hear the man who entered the sanctuary from the side door.

"Is anything wrong, ma'am?"

At first it seemed Talitha didn't hear him, but she finally offered, "No," in a soft tone. She continued to stare at the ornament, her fingers fumbling around its shape. "No, nothing at all. In fact, I think something may be right." This time her words were a little more audible.

The kind man had no idea what this woman was talking about, but he knew this was a house of solace and refuge, and whatever was in her heart and on her mind for the moment, she was in the right place.

Time began to move again as Talitha looked up at the man and smiled. "I'm sorry. I was so taken aback by this ornament that it seemed to whisk me away to my childhood for a moment." She gave a small sigh. "You see, when I was a little girl, I took piano lessons, and I used to sit and play with one hand while holding my doll with the other. If you'll look closely, you'll even see that this little girl on the ornament has the same color hair as me."

The man stepped closer to get a peek at the ornament in her hand to see that Talitha was right. "That's amazing."

She gave another small sigh. "The 'real' amazing thing is that the first hymn I learned was *Church in the Wildwood* and I would sit and play it every afternoon, sometimes with one hand and the doll in the other, or sometimes with both hands and the doll in my lap." Her eyes moved back down to the ornament.

Now it was the man's turn to stand spellbound. "That's my favorite hymn."

"Mine, too." Talitha looked back up at him. "In fact, it's the only hymn that I remember very well. I haven't attended church regularly in a long time and I've forgotten most of the hymns I learned as a child. But my grandparents loved it, too, so it was just recently played at my grandfather's funeral service."

The man gave her a consoling nod accompanied by a comforting smile. "Do you still remember how to play it?"

"I don't know. I haven't touched a piano in years. That

went by the wayside at about the same time going to church did."

"You're welcome to try." The man extended his arm to point toward the piano. "It's page 367 in the book."

She moved to the piano and placed the ornament on the music rack as she leafed through the pages to find the right number for *Church in the Wildwood.* Talitha began to pick out the melody with her right hand, then finally placed both hands on the keys and let them roam the keys. *How good this feels.* She had forgotten how much she actually enjoyed playing the piano.

Soon the missed notes were turning into beautiful strains of harmony as she imagined her grandparents listening to her. She could hear her grandmother's voice in the distance singing every word.

"We sing that hymn here a lot, but many times we change the words so that instead of singing about the little brown church in the lane, we sing about the little white church in the lane."

Talitha gave a slight chuckle as she envisioned the church full of people on a Sunday morning, all singing about their own little white church. "That's really special." With only his brief insight, she could sense a Power strong at work in this place.

"I didn't mean to disturb you," the man said, "so I'll get back to work. Thank you for playing the hymn for me."

"My pleasure. I might have to go out and buy a piano now."

"You're welcome to come here and play this one anytime."

"Oh, I appreciate that, but I don't live around here. I'm only taking a tour of Cedar Mountain while in the area."

"I don't live in the area, either, but Preacher has meant a lot to me. My wife came here and when I finally visited, I knew this was the place I was supposed to be."

Talitha gave an understanding smile. She had no idea how to respond to his words, for the church had not been her home for many years.

"Well, I'd better get back to work. I took the day off so that I could take care of a few things around here that needed fixin' up. Preacher said he'd like to have a red door, so I thought it would be nice to have it painted when he comes in on Sunday morning. Besides, I kind'a wanted to have a day alone."

"And here I am bothering you. Let me get out of here and let you get back to work."

"You weren't no bother. I think God sent you here today."

A puzzled look spread across Talitha's face. *Why would God send me here, in the middle of nowhere?*

"You've sure made me feel lots better today."

"Thank you. Thank you very much." She looked at him for a moment. "You've made me feel a lot better, too." *Perhaps God did send me here today. I've heard of those kinds of things happening, but I thought they were only someone's imagination.*

"My name's Raymond. We'd be pleased to have you come back here on Sunday and play the piano for us."

Talitha laughed. She had no intention of being in Cedar Mountain on Sunday. She had no intention of going to church on Sunday. *And* she had no intention of playing the piano in front of people on this Sunday or any other Sunday. "Thanks for the invitation, but I'll be long gone by Sunday. I'm a writer, and I'm looking for a place to stay where I can sit back and relax while I work."

"There's lots of places around here."

"I'll remember that." She placed the ornament back on its branch and started toward the freshly-painted red door. "Oh, and by the way, my name's Talitha. Talitha Slagle."

"Come back anytime," Raymond called out as he waved and went back down a side hallway where he was "fixin' up" things.

Once outside, Talitha decided to take a walk around the church that she had learned was the second-oldest one in Transylvania County. *I wonder if Mickey's cane ever walked here.*

She took a turn to the side of the sanctuary opposite the parking lot and spotted a small cemetery. *I love old cemeteries. They're always full of stories.* Talitha couldn't resist the urge to go exploring through the old tombstones, trying to connect the families together in her mind.

The first tombstone was fairly new and extremely modern compared to some of the others in the small plot. There was no name on the back side, so she went to the front and gasped. Talitha wasn't sure if the gasp came from the fact that the person named on the huge chunk of granite was still alive, or that etched in the stone was merely the word, "PREACHER."

There was a concrete bench nearby, so she took a seat where she could stare at the large stone. The last name was etched in the top of the stone, and Pat's name was beside his, but the only given name for him was, "PREACHER."

"The church did that for them because they've been so good for us here," Talitha heard Raymond say behind her.

Now she was even more shocked, for she knew that tombstones of this size weren't cheap. But to have an entire community to remember you only as "Preacher," that was quite a tribute. She had only had the opportunity to see this man in Kelly's with his bowl of chili. *But what was it he said? He only goes there to be with his friends, not because of the food.* She walked back to stand in front of the marker. *It's all about the people.*

It wasn't until that moment that Talitha remembered the last time she'd been in a cemetery. *Recently, at Grandfather's service.* A dampness began to form around her eyes as she turned to move on to the other stones in the plot.

She read each name aloud, as if that somehow made the lives of the people buried here more real to her. There were infants, children, young adults, middle-aged adults and older adults – all placed beside other deceased family members. *And most of them related to each other, it appears,* she noted, recalling Randy's words about how they had to go off the mountain to marry outside the family. Joke or not, they all seemed to be connected as in-laws, if nothing else.

"Denver," she said, reading the name on the stone near the back of the small cemetery. She turned to see if Raymond was still behind her. "This is the man they told me all about at Kelly's. They've been rattling off tales about him every time I've gone there."

"Yes, Denver was quite a character. I remember the day he got conviction. I was here. Do you know that man really did change completely that day? I never saw him curse again, nor touch another drop of liquor."

Talitha looked at Raymond, then back down at the stone. She had not heard that story about the man buried here. "You mean to tell me that people really *can* change in the blinking of an eye?"

"They can. Most don't because they have to grow in the faith. But this man did. Changed immediately. Never saw anything to beat it."

"Look! He was a WWII veteran."

"Yep. Got wounded over there. He was one tough guy. I don't remember exactly what happened to him, but I heard tell that it would have killed anyone else."

"Huh," Talitha muttered, slowly walking back toward the front door of the church.

Did God really bring me here today? Why would He bring me here? I'm a good person. How is going to church going to make me any better, or make me treat people differently?

She stood and looked at the red doors.

"I painted them crimson red because Preacher said you enter the church through the blood of Christ," Raymond explained, noticing her stare.

Talitha nodded her head and walked toward the car.

"You're welcome to come on Sunday and play the piano again. Everyone would love to hear you. That was a real blessing."

"Thanks!" she waved. *Blessing? Now that's a word I've never been called before.*

Raymond went back into the building and Talitha sat in her car for a few minutes, thinking of the church with the red doors, its history and how it had touched the lives of many people. *Including Denver.*

Is it supposed to change my life, too?

Chapter 8

It wasn't until Talitha started to make a left turn back onto Reasonover Road that she remembered the realtor's mention of Modena Brendle. Her hands instinctively switched directions with the steering wheel in search of the woman with all the stories of this magical place.

The pavement ended just past the church and Reasonover narrowed into a rough and bumpy dirt road that eventually dwindled into little more than a grown-over path. She recalled hearing Randy's tales of a place called Moonshine Cave, hidden back in the woods somewhere off this road. "Hidden so far back that most people who lived here all their lives don't even know where it is," he'd informed her.

Her image of Mickey's cane crossed her mind again as she pondered over whether it had ever combed these woods and found the cave. *Or Square Oak or Long Rock or Dan's Camp*, she wondered, recalling other places of interest Randy and Doug had mentioned.

It wasn't long before the path became so full of overgrown brush that she could no longer navigate her car through it. *This has to be it.* Her eyes peered into the distance trying to find a cabin or house. Talitha opened the car door, but then remembered the realtor's warning to make sure the woman knew of her presence before getting out.

"Hello," she yelled, hearing her voice echo through the mountains. Getting no response, she tried again. "Hello, is anyone home?" Talitha decided to walk into the woods, thinking that Modena might then hear her call. She slammed the car's door, but before she had time to take even one step, a gun fired off into the air.

Talitha grabbed the door handle and tried to get back in, but forgot she had, as usual, hit the lock button when she got out. She fumbled with the remote in an effort to open the door.

"Mrs. Brendle?" she yelled, hoping to buy a little time. "I'm looking for Mrs. Modena Brendle."

"Who sen'cha?" Talitha heard coming through the trees.

"A lady at the Mountain Living Realty Company back down the street."

There was no response.

"And Randy Heath down at Kelly's restaurant," Talitha added, remembering the stories that had been passed down by the old mountain woman.

"Randy, you say?" came a questioning voice.

This is worse than any job interview could ever be! "Yes, ma'am."

"You know Randy Heath?"

"Yes, ma'am." Talitha was standing frozen, still clutching onto the door handle.

"What's his grandmother's name?"

God, what is this? You'd think I was trying to get into Fort Knox.

Worse! came the booming voice she'd been hearing for the past few days.

She ignored the voice and strained to remember the stories Randy had told about his grandmother taking him fishing. *What was her name?* Not until she stopped to focus on that one word did Talitha realize how badly her knees were knocking.

"God, please help me," she whispered, hoping the tremble all over her body would stop.

Libby, came the voice.

Libby? Where did that word come from? Talitha wondered silently. *And what does it have to do with my body shaking and my knees knocking?*

"That's it! Libby!" Suddenly Talitha was screaming at the top of her lungs. "Her name was Libby!"

It wasn't but a few seconds until she heard the brush moving and saw a face appear in front of her.

"Land's sakes! What in tarnation are ya doing way out here? You're certainly not from these parts." The elderly woman turned her head to the side and gave a big spit, wiping the tobacco juice that dripped on her chin with a paper napkin. "But if Randy sen'cha, or ya knowed Mrs. Libby, why then, you're welcome.

C'mon up to the house with me."

Talitha followed the woman, this time feeling like she'd left Camelot and entered the Wilderness Trail, except a century earlier. Tree limbs hid the house, which was actually little more than two rooms and a lean-to in the woods, and appeared to have been there for several generations. Modena climbed the rock steps and sat down on the front porch, which too had seen better days, in one of the two rockers, with the visitor following suit.

"Wha'chur name and what brings ya here?"

"My name is Talitha Slagle. And no, I'm not from around here, but my grandfather was from the mountains of North Carolina. Does that count?"

"How'd ya wind up gettin' here? I ain't never had nobody find their way back here less'un they's lookin' fer trouble. Say, you don't work fer the guv'ment, do's ya?"

The visitor laughed and quickly added, not wanting to take another chance with the shotgun, "No, no. I'm a writer. I worked for a newspaper."

"That's dang near 'bout as bad." Another huge spit of tobacco juice hit the ground. "Say, didn't nobody sen'cha out here's to write nothing, did they?"

"Oh, no, ma'am. I happened to be visiting here in search of a place to live and went into Kelly's to eat. Randy and his father told me all about Cedar Mountain and their stories, of course, included you."

"You comin' here t'write for our paper?"

"No, ma'am. I'm hopefully going to be writing articles for magazines."

"I'uz supposed t'be in a magazine once. Someone from a

farm journal came out here to see how we raised so much corn, but ever'body sent him hoppin.' Didn't trust 'im." The elderly woman gave a chuckle and spit all at the same time. "Say, you ever read our *Transylvania Times?*"

"I hadn't until today. Randy showed me the article about Mack's Place."

"Yep, Mrs. Corn. I sure hate t'see the store close. She'd been there fer a long time."

"It was sad to ride by there today and see the 'Closed' sign hanging on the door."

"Yep. That place's been her life, all the way through the last half of the twentieth-century, and right on into the twenty-first. Reckon she'll git t'sit around like me now."

Talitha nodded, unsure what to say.

"I do like t'read the 'Cedar Mountain News' in the *Transylvania Times.* They's some woman named Linda Young who writes it. She's a good writer and tells some funny stories. I hear tell she ain't from here, neither."

"I'll have to take a look at her column."

"Yep." The tobacco hit the makeshift spittoon, nothing but an old orange juice can with the top cut off, on the porch. "Ya know, my pa raised me and my fifteen brothers and sisters in this house. Course it wasn't as nice then. It had holes between all the boards and through the floor. We used to watch the chickens underneath us, pecking all around the ground for anything that might drop through from the kitchen. The dogs 'un cats had 'nuff sense to know us young'un's always sticking scraps in our pockets fer 'em."

Time passed quickly, although for Talitha it seemed to stand still as she listened to tales of growing up in a large family, a much different lifestyle from what she was accustomed, but one that closely related that of her grandfather. When she finally glanced down at her watch and realized how late it had become, she swiftly stood from the chair and apologized for taking up the better part of the elderly woman's afternoon.

"Won'cha stay a spell un have some supper? I'd be mighty proud to have ya."

"Thank you, Mrs. Brendle." The invitation was quite un-expected, but Talitha felt it more rude to refuse it than to take up more of the woman's time. "I'd love to share a bite of supper with you."

"Pshaw, don't call me Mrs. Brendle. Why, my old man's been gone so long I don't even 'member what it was like to be a Missus. You can call me Modena."

The elderly woman moved to the door and opened a warped rickety screen, then turned the antique handle that still locked with a skeleton key. Talitha followed her inside and saw what could have easily been a museum of mountain life. Rows of shelves, holding canning jars of green beans and tomatoes, lined the walls. A couple of chairs and a sofa, covered with afghans and large pieces of fabric, sat in the room that was a shared kitchen, dining room and den. A wooden table and chairs, which had ob-viously been handcrafted by Modena's father and brothers, held jars of honey and jellies, also a product of the land.

"Now you say your grandfather was from the mountains?" Modena opened several jars of canned vegetables and made dough for cornbread and biscuits.

Talitha made herself at home in one of the wooden dining

chairs and watched the elderly woman swiftly throw a meal together. "Yes, ma'am. He grew up in Haywood County, right on the side of a mountain, in a little community called Balsam. I loved all the stories he'd tell me about growing up there. He died several weeks ago." Talitha decided to omit the part about the inheritance. "I decided that I'd like to be closer to where he was raised."

"You won't be sorry. It's good t'hear tell of somebody who's still got respect fer their elders. That's why I like Randy so much. He still respects the land and the people. Most of the folks from round here do, but it's all them "summer people" that comes in here and tries to take over. I don't have no problem with anybody comin' in here, but they oughtn't be tryin' to change our ways."

Talitha wasn't at all surprised by the timing of the last spit, which was into a smaller can in the corner of the kitchen by the back door.

"Didn't they come here cause it wuz diff'rent anyways?" Modena asked, in a like manner of Randy, whose questions were more like statements than phrases requiring answers.

The visitor was touched by both the woman's wisdom and her opinion.

"Yes, ma'am. I once heard that a traveler is someone who goes places to see things that are different, and then complains when they are."

A big smile broke across Mrs. Brendle's face. "Ya ought a write a story 'bout that saying. That'd be a good'un."

"Thanks! I might just do that." *And build the story around you.* But Talitha knew that now was neither the time nor place to broach that subject.

Modena poured the contents of all the pans into pottery

bowls, and placed the biscuits and cornbread into two baskets. She refused to let Talitha help her with setting the table or carrying the food to the table.

When the elderly woman took a seat, which was no doubt in a chair that had been hers for several decades, she immediately bowed her head. "Dear Lord, thank Ya fer this day and fer this food and for bringing Miss Talitha Slagle here. Bless this food and us to thy intended use. Amen."

"Ya can commence to eatin' now," offered Modena.

Talitha filled her plate with beans, peas and corn and took a piece of cornbread. *I'll save the biscuits and honey for dessert.* "This is delicious," she blurted after the first bite. "Thank you for inviting me."

"Wait'll ya see what's fer dessert. I made a fresh apple pie right 'fore ya come."

So much for the biscuits and honey. Guess there's no such thing as low-carb eating around here. She looked at the face of Mrs. Modena Brendle. *But then, she probably works off every extra calorie,* Talitha reasoned, seeing that most everything in sight had been made at the hands of the elderly woman.

After a few minutes of silence, she ventured to question something that had been puzzling her all afternoon. "Why is this place called Cedar Mountain? I only saw a couple of cedar trees, and they weren't very big."

"Ya ever heard of the Biltmore House?"

"Yes."

Modena chewed her mouthful of supper, taking her own sweet time, and looking as if there were no one sitting across the table from her. She shoveled another huge spoonful of beans into her mouth, ignoring the fact that Talitha was staring at her in eager anticipation of a further explanation of the name of Cedar Mountain.

"I've heard of the Biltmore House."

"I heared ya," Modena answered, chugging down another huge gulp of coffee. She took a couple more bites, again washing them down with large mouthfuls of coffee.

"What does the Biltmore House have to do with Cedar Mountain?"

"Years ago, a trucking company come in there and cut down all the cedar trees."

Talitha saw the fork piled with food moving toward the elderly woman's mouth again. "And?" she practically screeched, trying to first get an answer. Finally, out of desperation, she concluded, "And they took all the trees to the Biltmore House?"

"Yep." The fork's contents dumped into Modena's mouth.

The visitor watched the woman slowly chewing. *Good God, at this rate I'll be older than her before I ever find out all the stories of Cedar Mountain!* "Did they plant the trees at the estate?" she asked, unsuccessfully trying to be patient.

Modena reared her head back and laughed. Talitha had no idea what the woman found so funny about the question other than the fact that she was being strung along. About the time it hit her that the trees couldn't be replanted if they'd been cut down, Modena finished eating and gave her the rest of the information.

"They're all in the floor over there. George Vanderbilt contracted with that lumber company t'cut all them trees that once lined our beautiful mountains fer his floor in that big ole house. Don't know what he needed such a big house fer anyway."

After hearing the rest of the story, Talitha found it hard to believe that Modena had been able to laugh at all about it, even though the humor had come from her comment about replanting the trees. She also deduced that mealtime was for eating and not talking. To this mountain woman, it was a necessity, not merely a time of social interaction.

The dessert of deep-dish apple pie took Talitha back, as had the banana pudding, to the kitchen of her grandmother. *Sure wish I had all these recipes. But then, when would I ever use them?*

Once the table had been cleared and the leftovers put away, Modena sat in a chair beside the sofa and shared more of the history of Cedar Mountain. Characters that had already been introduced by Randy, and new ones described by this "Queen of the Mountain," came alive as Talitha let her mind visualize all the information she was receiving.

"We did have a professor what lived up here fer awhile. He wuz always a little strange. Never got married, that 'un." Modena shelled a pecan into a round wooden bread bowl that had obviously had decades of use.

In fact, Talitha couldn't help but wonder if it was one of those kitchen wares that had been passed down from the elderly woman's mother. *Or even grandmother!*

"He did ask a woman out one time. They went t'one o' them summer plays at the Transylvania Music Theater in Brevard." Another handful of pecan meat fell into the pan. "He went out at intermission and stood looking up at the stars, and then he walked home." Modena gave a loud sigh that slightly resembled a short belly laugh. "Seems like he fergot about 'er and left 'er there."

"I guess that was the end of that relationship."

Modena broke into a fit of laughter.

Talitha found it most odd at the way folks around here left a topic up in the air, like a mental way of carrying them back to that place and time.

"I liked the times ever'body on the mountain took off down t'Bonnie's Hill when it snowed. My, oh my, at the good times we had down there. Ya ever met Randy's brother, Michael?" Before Talitha had a chance to respond, Modena continued., "Why, them two boys wuz more fun than a barrel o' monkeys." Another short belly laugh emitted between phrases. "Huh, why havin' that Michael 'round wuz like having two whole barrels o' monkeys. Boy, could he make ever'body laugh. Still does, too. Ya ought'a hear him cut loose at our annual Cedar Mountain Auction."

"When is that?"

"It's usually in August, I think. But some one o' them months when all the summer people's here. Ever'body brings a covered dish down to the Community Center and Michael, who we all call the Mayor of Cedar Mountain, gets up and entertains ever'body while playing the auctioneer. He's real good and don't nobody git outta there without laughing up a storm."

Talitha loved hearing Modena tell the stories. *If Michael's any funnier than this lady, I don't know if I can stand it.*

"Anyways, them boys and their friends would take the big ole Coca-Cola signs that hung up on the stores and fly down Bonnie's Hill. One year it got so cold that it froze on top o' the snow and they really could fly. S'wonder one of 'em didn't git kilt." Modena shook her head sideways. "But all us in the older generation would build a big ole bonfire t' keep warm and watch them young'uns havin' a good time. Always brought back mem'ries from when I'uz a child."

"Modena, why don't you write something for the newspaper? I'll bet you could write all kinds of interesting stories."

"Pshaw! I'll leave the writin' t'you. But'chu come back here some time. I'll tell ya plenty o'stories."

"Thank you, Mrs. Brendle . . . Modena. I'll take you up on that." *And I'll wait until then to ask if she'd mind if I send any of them into a magazine.*

Talitha carefully made her way back to the car, pushing branches out of her way as she went. *Reasonover Road was a real experience. The only thing I missed was Denver's house and I'll find that the next time.* She turned the ignition. *Surely Mickey's cane had made Mrs. Modena's acquaintance. How could anybody live here and not know of her?*

Then the *real* question hit her – a question she'd forgotten totally about until this minute.

Did God answer my question about Randy's grandmother's name or was that my memory? I don't remember realizing what the name was before I started screaming it. Talitha's mind was in such a fog that she had no recollection of those few minutes in the woods before Modena came to greet her. *Maybe it's simply that I was so terrified that my subconscious took over,* she reasoned, determined to find a logical solution.

Chapter 9

"Yep, that's sure 'nuff how the road got it's name."

Talitha was humored by Randy's explanation of the day the state crew came by and asked Denver what they should call his road, based on any outstanding characters or places that had made history on it.

"He just reared back, rubbed his chin and said, 'I'll have to reason over that one.'"

"Reasonover Road," she smiled as she said the name of the road aloud. Then she burst into a fit of laughter. "Wait a minute. Don't tell me that's how Tutherside, on the way to Pretty Place, got it's name, too. Denver, instead of saying, 'To the other side,' pronounced it as 'tutherside?'"

"You got it. Tutherside is directly on the other side of the mountain from him."

"I love it. Are there any other cool road names around here?"

"Don't know about road names," interjected Regina, "but they say they used pigs to figure out how to cut the roads through here from Greenville, South Carolina."

"What . . . how?" asked Talitha. "I thought pigs were supposed to be fairly dumb animals."

"The farmers would have to come over the mountain to take their pigs to market," Doug explained. "The pigs would instinctively take the shortest route to get down and around the mountain, so the road crews decided to follow the farmers and their pigs to see the best way."

"This is unbelievable. I've read about the cows being the measurement for the tunnels on Highway 191 over in Henderson County. And how the horses' rear ends were the measurement for railroads. But now you're telling me that pigs were the engineers for all these mountain roads? Talk about engineers! So you wonder why all those office people get paid so much money."

"You're right!" exclaimed Regina. "They should have paid the farmers."

"Or the pigs!" laughed Talitha. She was elated that she was called a regular this morning by Randy and Regina the minute she came through the door and now they were both sitting at her booth sharing more stories.

Doug walked out of the kitchen. "You're here two days in

a row? You really *are* a regular!" He joined the threesome in between seating other customers and clearing tables.

Talitha shared her experience of the day before at Blue Ridge Baptist Church.

"You know," Randy said, "Preacher was there for thirty-five years and then left to go somewhere else. He was there back when I was growing up."

"Kelly's is where they came looking for him when they asked him to come the second time and preach," added Regina. "They knew they loved him and wanted him back."

"And that he ate here every day," Randy chuckled.

"I couldn't believe it when I saw his tombstone in the cemetery." Talitha told them about her tour of the cemetery. "I loved it when I found Denver's gravesite."

"Yep, old Denver. We sure had some good times, me and Michael, at his house. Especially on the days when it would snow, or we'd have to miss school on account of the weather."

"Hey, Randy," asked Regina, "remember that old tombstone that's out beside Solomon Jones Road? We used to ride our bikes down there when we were kids, and always wondered whose it was."

"But it wasn't a person," Randy explained to Talitha. "It was a horse that belonged to Grandma's brother."

"Yeah, Uncle Emerson loved his horse so much that he buried it beside the road at the old home place."

"I think he loved that horse more than he loved his kids."

"Uncle Emerson's the one with the good black walnut pound cake recipe, right?" Talitha asked, trying to assimilate the information she'd been given earlier.

"That's right," smiled Randy.

"You're really catching on," Regina added with encouragement.

Doug stopped as he strode by the booth. "That wasn't a horse. It was only a pony."

His comment brought a chuckle to Talitha. She had sudden visions of playing the Gossip Game in Sunday School as a small child. It had also been a favorite of her second grade teacher. She could even remember how all the children would anxiously look down the line after they'd whispered in their neighbor's ear to hear what ridiculous thing would spew out of the mouth of the person at the end.

"I could sit here and listen all day, but I've got to get back to work. You three have given me way too many writing ideas for one day. It will take me all week to draft my stories from today's visit."

"Why don't you come over to my house and have supper with me and the wife?" invited Randy. "We're having homemade vegetable soup with fried okra and Mama's creamed corn on the side. Hope's making some of her famous corn cakes."

"Sounds too good to pass up," accepted Talitha. "Here's my cell phone number. Give me a call about five minutes before it's ready. Can I bring anything?"

"Just your pen and paper," instructed Doug. He'd come to appreciate the fact that this newcomer took such an interest in the history of the community, so much so that she wanted to tell the rest of the world about it.

"You just make sure you don't make us sound so good that the 'summer people' take over," teased Randy.

Chapter 10

There were numerous fears manifesting themselves inside Talitha as she pulled into the parking lot of Blue Ridge Baptist Church, but the greatest one was that the Christmas tree and all the decorations would be gone. She was sure that one thing would hold her attention during the service and help distract her from the other underlying excuses of why she shouldn't go to church, so she was thrilled when she opened the crimson door and to her surprise, the lights were twinkling on the tree.

Talitha wanted to sneak up to the altar and see if the ornament that had drawn her back this morning was still there, but she decided to go to the ladies' room before people had time to get out of Sunday School. When she turned on the light, she saw that the walls had been painted a beautiful shade of orchid, and there was a Thomas Kincade wallpaper border surrounding the room to give it an aura of cozy homes and lighthouses. The room had been carefully decorated, down to the smallest details, obviously with love and care.

As she passed the nursery on her way back to the sanctuary, Talitha stopped to stick her head in the door. "Excuse me," she said as the teacher glanced up at her. "I didn't mean to disturb you. It's just that I was so impressed with the ladies' room that I had to see the nursery."

"You're not interrupting anything. We redid this room for the children not long ago," the lady offered.

One of the children looked up at Talitha when she heard a voice in the doorway. "I'm going to get a Happy Meal."

"You are?" Talitha asked. *How many times did I eat at McDonald's as a child? Only we didn't have Happy Meals back then. But boy, how I loved those burgers and fries and strawberry milkshakes!* She fondly remembered when the home of the Golden Arches first opened on Independence Boulevard in Charlotte, and her parents would take her there after church on Sundays.

I grew up in church. Why and when did I stop going? Talitha wondered, thinking back to when her absence from church began.

When Talitha got back to the sanctuary, there was already a couple seated in a pew, so she decided not to examine the tree.

"You must be the piano player," said the man.

Talitha looked at him, quite startled. "I guess you could

say that."

"I hear you're going to play a special for us today," added the woman.

Talitha smiled sheepishly. "Oh, well, I guess I could if I had to." The wheels in her mind began to furiously turn while she tried to think of some old gospel hymns that she could whip out from her childhood. Being the organized person she was, she sat down in the second pew – close behind the piano – and on her trusty pad that stayed in her purse from years of journalism, began to jot down the names of a few titles she thought these people might like as she combed through the well-worn pages of a hymnbook.

The woman who had been in the nursery entered the sanctuary, the little girl who was already thinking about lunch behind her. She walked up to the tree, removed the ornament that Talitha had spotted two days earlier, and quietly handed it to her.

"You must be Raymond's wife." *How else could she have known of my attraction to the ornament.* Talitha glanced at the pen and paper in her hand. *But then, these people knew I played the piano.*

"Yes, I am."

Talitha reached out her hand. "I'm Talitha Slagle. Sorry I didn't introduce myself earlier. I didn't think about you being the wife of the man I met Friday." After they shook hands, she looked down at the ornament in her left hand and ran her fingers of her right hand around it, much like she had done when she first saw it. "I take it he mentioned my attraction to this ornament?"

"Yes, he did. He came straight home after he finished the door and told me all about you, the ornament, and your playing. Meeting you was a real blessing to him."

"I'm the one who was blessed. When he invited me to come today, I had no intention of being here. But during the course of the past couple of days, I knew this was where God wanted me to be on this Sabbath."

"We're so glad you're here," welcomed Raymond, who had now joined their conversation. Then he turned to the man seated in the pew. "Morning. How're you doing today?"

"I'm kicking," answered the man. "I won't say how high, but I'm kicking."

Talitha found these local expressions most endearing.

It wasn't long before Preacher walked in, followed by Pat, and they took their place on the front pew. Another man came in behind them, walked up to the podium and welcomed "the flock" then made the week's announcements. "Do we have any birthdays?"

No one moved or said anything.

"How about an anniversary? I know we have an anniversary here."

Talitha watched as Preacher and Pat got up and walked, hand in hand, to the altar table at the front of the church. The minister reached into his shirt pocket, took out a dollar and placed it in the top of a little wooden church bank that looked exactly like the sanctuary building.

"How many years, Preacher?" asked the man making the announcements.

"Forty-nine years," answered the couple, proudly, at the same time.

"And we'll make it another one if she doesn't give out on me," Preacher snickered.

Pat grinned and looked up at her husband, then out to the congregation. "If he doesn't give out on me!"

Laughter rang throughout the sanctuary, bouncing off the poplar walls. Talitha loved the show of emotions in this place. People were not at all intimidated or ashamed to share either their burdens or their praises in this place. *They truly do lay everything at the foot of the cross*, she thought.

The celebrating couple sat back down and the man behind the podium called out the hymns for the morning. The congregation sang three hymns, all of which Talitha had heard as a child at her grandfather's church. The final one, *Just a Little Talk with Jesus*, brought back all sorts of memories. She had heard it at regular intervals during her entire life, even during the years she strayed from the church. Being a favorite of her grandfather's, he would sing it all the time, no matter whether he was happy or sad. It always amazed her how her grandfather could sing the dominant bass part of the chorus, and then come in all the other voice parts, too.

As they sang the final words of the chorus, "Just a little talk with Jesus makes it right," it struck Talitha that the words were more than just a hymn. They truly were a prayer, an utterance for Christ to come into these peoples' lives and make things anew, a plea that some people only strived to do on New Year's. *Like me*, Talitha sadly confessed. But these people, as had her grandfather, obviously strived to make that petition each and every day.

Talitha missed the first few words of the morning's prayer while thinking of how each day was indeed a new day. "Each and every one filled with blessings," she caught from a man in the pews who'd been called upon to pray.

The minute the "Amen" was uttered, Preacher stepped up to the pulpit. "Today is the first Sunday of a new year. You are going down a path that you've never been before, and God isn't going to lead you anywhere that He isn't going to go with you."

Talitha was prepared to listen intently on the words of the man revered by so many. His learning and understanding had come from reading and application of the Bible, not years of classes. Yet, his words rang as true as any minister's she had ever heard.

However, his words stopped and he looked her in the eyes. "Today, we have a visitor. I believe the Lord called this woman here today. And now, I'm going to ask Sister Talitha to come up and play a few songs on the piano for us."

The visitor was dumbfounded. *Now? Come up there and play now? Now that you have everyone's attention.* She was totally unaware of the applause, indications of support, coming from the pews until she stood to move to the piano.

Where's my list? she panicked, sitting at the piano. Then she breathed a sigh of relief. *Thank goodness, someone's looking out for me.* The hymnbook on the music rack was still turned to *Church in the Wildwood.*

Her fingers began to hunt and peck for the keys, much like they had done on Friday. *Pretend you're playing for your grandfather, Talitha.* She had no idea where the voice had come from, *it's probably the voice of the One who left the hymnbook open for me,* but she didn't care. Suddenly, she forgot about the people congregated in the pews and she let go and let her fingers glide across the keys as they had done on a word processor for so many years.

When she stood from the piano, there was another burst of applause.

"Thank you, Sister Talitha, for sharing your abundant talent with us today. Pat and I met this young woman down at Kelly's, but we had no idea she could play the piano until Raymond called us up on Friday and told us about how he'd met her here that afternoon. We want to thank the Lord for bringing her our way this morning."

Talitha's embarrassment completely dissipated, for all she could sense was the pride her grandfather would have felt had he been there to hear her. She missed most of the rest of the sermon, even though she tried to concentrate on Preacher's words. But it seemed there was a sermon of her own going on inside her head.

When the final "Amen" had been said following the benediction, "the flock" crowded around Talitha, thanking her for sharing her gift and encouraging her to do it again. Preacher and Pat made an effort to introduce her to everyone.

"This is the only person I ever baptized before they were born," Preacher stated, placing his arm around a boy of about ten or eleven. "I baptized his mother when she was carrying this young man, and I got to baptize him again this past summer."

By the time Talitha walked out the crimson door, she'd heard stories from practically everyone who'd attended Blue Ridge Baptist that morning. She knew all about the McGaha family for which the old Methodist Church she'd admired, McGaha Chapel on Highway 276, had been named. "A good number of the family goes to First United Methodist in Brevard, but there's a bunch of us and we're scattered all over the mountain," shared one lady.

"My mother's the woman in that big newspaper article back there on the wall," boasted another lady, proud of her church and her Christian heritage.

"We hope you'll come back again," pleaded the last man out the door behind her as he walked her to her car. "We'll be looking for you."

Talitha sat in her car for a few minutes after everyone else had left and stared at the small ornament that she'd pulled back out of her coat pocket. "No spot is so dear to my childhood," she sang, recalling the weathered brown wood of the McGaha Chapel and also in the photo of the old Baptist church hanging on the wall, "as the little brown church in the dale."

Chapter 11

"Hey, Talitha," Randy called out when he saw Kelly's newest "regular" walk through the door. "Figured ya'll must'a got all fired up today since Preacher and Pat was so late, and you wasn't here yet."

"It was her fault," Preacher winked at their guest. "The fire department had to come out. She set the keys on fire."

"Tore that piano up, I'll tell you," Pat laughed.

"You play the piano?" Randy inquired of Talitha.

"I used to play a bit, back when I was a kid."

"You should'a heard her," answered Pat. "I'll say she can."

"That's good because I have someone who wants to meet you, and she's quite a musician, too," Randy said, pointing Talitha toward a corner booth. "Talitha, this is Ellyn and Phill Masterson. I told them about you and they're very anxious to meet you."

"Likewise, I'm sure," she nodded. As Talitha took the opposite seat in the booth from the couple, she saw Ellyn's face. "I'm sorry, I didn't recognize you at first."

"That's quite alright. So we meet again."

"Do you two know each other?" the puzzled husband asked.

"Talitha stopped by the office to get directions to Reasonover Road," Ellyn explained. "Only then I didn't know her name."

"And I take it you found it?" This time Phill's words were directed to Talitha.

"Oh, yes. It is the most wonderful place I've ever been on the face of the earth."

"Ah! Another person caught in the magical web of Cedar Mountain," he said in a poetic tone.

"I take it that happens fairly often from the way you made that comment," Talitha noted.

"Quite a bit," he admitted. "But I can't complain. That's what keeps Ellyn in business. I keep telling her not to get too busy. We don't want Cedar Mountain to lose that unpopulated charm."

"That's why he bought me the license tag that says, 'ITOOBUSY.' He wants me to remember that we want this place to stay the way it is."

"From what I understand," stated Talitha, "western North Carolina has become quite a resort area. I can remember when I was little and my grandparents bought a place in Maggie Valley, near their hometown of Balsam. Their intention was to use it as a vacation home." The stunned woman stopped and thought about her statement. *That was before most folks in Union County, or any of the rural areas, for that matter, had a vacation home. Why, Grandfather had money way back then. Why didn't I ever figure that out?*

She left her thoughts unattended and returned to the conversation. "My grandfather worked hard and didn't get much time for vacations. And when he heard about a family up in the mountains who needed a place to stay, he told one of his nephews, who kept an eye on it, to let them stay in the vacation home. 'We probably won't get to go more than twice a year. This family needs a place to stay all the year,' Granddaddy told Grandmommy."

Mrs. B came to take Talitha's order, then disappeared, leaving the threesome to get acquainted. "I understand you're a writer," began Ellyn.

"Yes, I am, and Randy says that you're a musician."

"I do play the viola. But it's been quite a while since I've picked up the instrument."

"I've always had a hidden desire to be a musician," admitted Talitha.

"And I've always possessed a hidden desire to be a writer," confessed Ellyn.

The two women wasted no time in comparing notes and learning they shared numerous similar interests.

"Where are you staying?" asked Phill.

"Right now, I'm staying in Edneyville with some friends. I'm looking for a small place somewhere in the mountains that is conducive to a writing atmosphere."

"What kind of place?" shot Ellyn, inquiring further into

the matter.

"I love porches. I do a lot of my writing outside. And I'd love a scenic view. I'm one of these writers that feels my place in nature."

By the time they'd finished eating, Ellyn and Phill had invited Talitha to their church to play the piano, and also told her about a cabin they rented in Cedar Mountain. And the writer had offered to write an article about Transylvania County's claim to fame as the "Land of the Falls."

"Thanks for the information. I might give you a call the next time I'm in the area." Talitha waved good-bye to her new acquaintances.

Randy took a seat in the booth with Talitha after the Masterson's left. "So did ya'll have a lot to talk about?"

"We sure did. Thanks for introducing me to them. I can't wait to see them again."

Doug brought over a plate of food and joined the party, which turned into another storytelling session of "the life and times of Cedar Mountain."

The restaurant closed at 2:00, but at 4:00, Talitha was still seated in her booth, Randy and Doug across the booth from her, and Regina and Thelma, Randy's mother, across the aisle at another booth. They were rattling off beloved family tales, one after the other. Talitha was rolling in laughter, realizing that this was the best she had felt in months, especially since the death of her grandfather. And sitting here listening to all these stories had brought about a healing from her divorce that months of support groups had not.

Her mind went back to listening to the yarn that Randy

was spinning. "Uncle Paul was the appointed dentist of Cedar Mountain. He had a pair of pliers that he used to pull his horse's teeth."

Talitha was gearing up for another bout of laughter.

"One day, Percy had a toothache he said was killing him. He walked down Reasonover to Uncle Paul's and told him to pull his tooth." Randy stopped long enough to laugh himself and look over at his dad. "Uncle Paul told the women folk to go back up on the hill, and he told Percy to go over and stand behind the forked dogwood tree.."

"The forked dogwood tree?" Talitha wondered aloud, unsure what a dogwood tree had to do with pulling teeth.

"He had to have something for leverage," explained Doug.

Talitha nodded her head that she understood as Randy went on with his tale, Thelma and Regina joining in the laughter.

"They gave Percy a shot of white lightnin' and told him to hold onto that tree. Uncle Paul laid hold o' that tooth, and jerked it right out. Percy yelled, 'Yeah, why don't you go ahead and pull the rest of 'em?' and Uncle Paul did. Then Percy took his pocket knife out and whittled himself a set of teeth right there, he did." And with that, Randy slammed his fist down on the wooden table as if to say, "The End."

The attentive listener loved their manner of telling stories. There was something about these mountain people; they all seemed to come equipped with the fine art of storytelling. *But then, that's how they've entertained themselves for years.* She began to wonder how far back some of their tales went.

Just as Talitha thought the two men were ready to pack up and go home, Randy started up with another story. "And talk about a woman who could fish. My Grandma could fish."

Libby. That would be Libby. I'll never forget that name again! she noted, remembering her introduction with Modena.

"She's the one who taught me to fish. She wuz gonna take me fishing one day, and I thought I had to have a fancy rod. I walked to her house and out she starts with this bamboo pole about fifteen feet long, and a string hanging down about this long." He separated his hands and held them approximately three feet apart. "That was the ugliest fishing pole I'd ever seen. 'Don't take that thing. Grandma,' I begged. 'That thing looks stupid.'

"She didn't pay me a bit of attention. Off we went down her road, her dragging that long, ugly pole behind her while I's hopin' nobody saw us."

The story, the images and the dialect of the story gave Talitha the impression that she was reading from a Mark Twain book rather than listening to someone relating real family stories.

"Thank you for an afternoon of entertainment. This has been the most delightful day I've had in I don't know how long."

"It was just as much fun for us," replied Thelma. "I get so busy back in that kitchen sometimes that I don't get time to think about all those old fun times. It was great to sit back and enjoy my family this afternoon."

"And I've never gotten to tell you directly, but the food here is wonderful. Maybe one day I'll be an 'official' member of the Gang."

Randy burst into laughter. "I don't know if you could handle that bunch. They get kind'a rowdy from time to time."

"Don't forget I grew up near Charlotte. I've seen plenty of rowdy."

"Ah, them city slickers don't hold a candle to us mountain folk."

Talitha looked at the four faces, new acquaintances, but seemingly old friends. "You know, I think you're right." She smiled. "You've already taught me many things."

"Just wait 'til you meet our brother, Michael. He's the 'real' rowdy one of the bunch," warned Regina.

"Michael?" asked Talitha. "I thought Modena said he's the Mayor of Cedar Mountain."

All four of the Heaths' howled with laughter.

"Yep, he's the Mayor alright," chuckled Randy.

"Cedar Mountain doesn't really have a mayor," Regina informed her. "They just say that about Michael because everybody knows him."

"Yeah, they know him alright," snickered Doug. "But I think he's more the 'town clown.'"

"So when do I get to meet this Michael?" inquired Talitha.

"Never, if you're lucky," joked Thelma.

Now I'm sure I'll have to come back here. This guy sounds like a real trip, and after all, I want to write travel features.

Chapter 12

The three-and-a-half hour return flight from Denver provided Talitha exactly enough time to pull her details together and write the final draft of her latest project. So far, she'd landed her first good article, for which she was paid expenses, and was scheduled to fly out again on the next morning, giving her barely enough time to do laundry, repack and change gears in preparation for another assignment.

Talitha turned on her cell phone as she hurriedly made her way toward the Charlotte airport's baggage claim. No more had the signal been picked up than the phone rang.

"Miss Slagle?"

She didn't readily recognize the voice. "Yes."

"Thank goodness I caught you. I've been dialing every ten minutes hoping to reach you. This is Mrs. Lafayette. I'm the woman in Louisville, Kentucky, whom you're scheduled to interview on Sunday."

"Oh, yes. How are you?"

"I'm fine, but terribly cold and snowed in. And it looks like we're going to get no relief over the next few days. I'm sorry, but we're going to have to postpone our event for Sunday. I hope this doesn't mess you up too much."

Talitha breathed a sigh of relief. "Oh, no, not at all. In fact, I'm walking through the airport now on my way home from a writing assignment. I was going to have to rush to get ready to leave again in the morning. This will actually give me a needed break."

"God does have a way of taking care of us, doesn't He?"

How is it that everyone I come in contact with lately has this perception? "So it appears." She failed to share her skepticism with the woman on the other end of the line. *Of course, I have been wishing I had turned down this trip. Did God take that as a prayer?*

Talitha realized the woman was still talking to her and had asked a question. "I'm sorry, my reception isn't the best. Could you repeat that?"

"Sure. Is there any way we could reschedule this story for April? Maybe around Easter?"

Easter? That's the day Randy told me they do the Easter Sunrise Service at Pretty Place. "I'm sorry, but I'm already committed for that day." Talitha quickly tried to think through her commitments in Cedar Mountain. "I'm also scheduled for another interview on the following week. I think the last Sunday of the month might be a possibility. Of course, I'll have to get back to you once I check my calendar."

"I understand. But in the meanwhile, let's tentatively plan on the last Sunday in April. I'll wait to hear back from you."

"Fine. I'll get back to you within the next day or so."

Was this God's way of looking out for me? I know I wanted to have the weekend to relax before leaving for my next article. But I never said a prayer.

Talitha tried to remember the last timewhen she had consciously prayed. It had been such a long while that she couldn't even recall it. *And I'm not going to waste anymore time thinking about it now.*

The loud buzzing of the horn indicating that the luggage from her flight had arrived blocked all thoughts as she watched for her bag. It wasn't until she had reached the satellite parking lot and was on her way toward the freeway that her thoughts returned to the subject of prayer. And not only the subject of prayer, but she found herself bubbling with excitement that she would be able to attend church at Cedar Mountain the next morning, then have lunch at Kelly's.

Drat! Talitha suddenly remembered that Kelly's was closed for a week-long remodeling project. *Oh well, at least I can find out where everyone has eaten all week. This will give me a chance to try out one of the other local restaurants.*

The minute Talitha was out of the airport, she grabbed her cell phone and swiftly dialed the ten digits. "Hi, Ellyn. This is Talitha Slagle, the writer who met you at Kelly's and your realty office."

"Hello, Talitha. How well I remember. Are you back in town?"

Talitha loved that question. "Town." That word that was assigned to many regions, but Cedar Mountain was not one that seemed to fit. "No, I've just flown into Charlotte and I'm on my way toward the mountains. I wanted to see if your cabin was rented for this week. I have some time to write and I'd love to spend it in Cedar Mountain."

"We begin our rentals next week. The lady who does the cleaning for us just finished getting the cabin ready for the season this morning. I'd love to have you stay in it. That would give it a chance to get broken in before the months of renters begin. "How long do you want to stay?"

"I need to be out next Sunday morning. I've got an assignment in Cabarrus County that afternoon. So, it would probably be better if I left on Saturday afternoon, a week from today."

"That's perfect. Our first renters are coming in on Sunday afternoon."

"What do I need to bring with me?"

"Just the same thing you'd take to a motel, and whatever food you'd like. Everything else is already in the cabin. And by the time you get here, we'll even have the sheets on the bed and the towels in the bathroom for you."

Talitha couldn't believe her ears. She knew it was no accident that she was staying in the red cabin she had admired both times she'd made the drive down Reasonover Road. It caught her eyes from the first time she'd rounded the curve that brought it into view. She was unsure as to whether its attraction was in the charm of the house or the tranquility of the small pond in front of it, but she fully intended to find out during the course of the next week.

It was early evening before Talitha finally arrived at the cabin, but as promised, the door was unlocked. The guest ventured inside and fumbled to find a light switch on the wall, thinking how it would have been to make this same entrance several years back when there had been no electricity here.

Fresh flowers, along with the keys and a note of welcome, had been placed on the kitchen table, which was long enough to seat a family of twelve. She busily wandered from room to room, looking for the best spot to light with her laptop.

What a far cry from my cramped desktop at the office! she smiled, noting all the nooks and crannies to hide and spread out her work materials. The smile grew into laughter as Talitha imagined this cabin as the desktop on a new computer, with all sorts of free workspace.

Every writer's dream!

She finished her expedition of the inside of the house and finally settled for the long, wooden kitchen table where she could spread her work from one end to the other. Once she had herself up and going with the story outline, she'd retreat to the loft, where the comfortable chair and small table, complete with a reading lamp, seemed like the dessert after the entrée. Then she could curl up under the flannel coverlet to read over the final draft and do any necessary last minute edits. *After that, I have a date with my favorite author!*

What a set up! This is like being on a permanent vacation.

The wheels of her mind were already racing with ideas for articles. The Masterson's cabin was a perfect setting for travel articles. Talitha had already made a mental list of possible places to consider, both for articles and for personal retreat, within an hour's drive of Cedar Mountain. *Not to mention that tomorrow morning, I can go outside to check all the natural points of inspiration.*

It was then that the houseguest felt an overpowering sense that coming to this hideaway was not her idea. *Nor merely a spot of inspiration for work.* Something inside, something very deep within her, developed an unsettling aura that this trip was a personal scavenger hunt exclusively for "one Talitha Slagle."

But what am I hunting for?

Chapter 13

The minute her feet hit the floor, accelerated by a burning desire to get outdoors and check out the scenery, Talitha realized why her grandfather had told numerous stories about having to get up at four in the morning to build a fire. *We're not in the low country anymore, Talitha!*

She remembered Ellyn's invitation from the day before to visit Rocky Hill Baptist Church. *I went to church several weeks ago. I'd really rather stay in and read until it gets warm enough to go outside. That loft is really cozy.*

She picked up her book on the way to the kitchen. *And*

probably toasty warm since heat rises.

The fresh flowers and the note on the table seemed to send Talitha's conscience soaring onto a guilt trip. *Ellyn was so gracious to let me come here at the last minute. The least I can do is give up an hour or two of my time to pacify her.* She turned on the coffee maker. *At least it won't kill you.*

Drip . . . drip . . . drip . . .

"And it might save you."

Why do I keep hearing that voice? It's a good thing I'm not spooked easily.

After she finished her coffee, getting in a couple of chapters in the cozy loft, Talitha got dressed for church. *I'll take a seat on the back pew. At least I'll have put in an appearance, and if things drag on, I can slip out early. I'll be sure and wave so she'll know I came.*

"Why don't you join the class down the hall?" invited Ellyn when she saw Talitha slip in the back door. "They have food."

"And I'm teaching," welcomed Phill, coming in behind the visitor. "Ellyn made a delicious coffee cake and I brought freshly squeezed OJ."

She walked in the door to excited greetings, similar to the ones she received several weeks earlier at Blue Ridge. *At least they're friendly.*

Talitha took a seat beside a woman who called her by name. "Phill and Ellyn told us you'd be here. We're so glad you decided to join us."

The visitor nodded, shocked that others knew more about her plans than she did.

An older woman, who carried herself well and had a demanding appearance, sat on the other side of Talitha. "What's your name, young lady?"

That's the first time I've been called "young lady" in a few years.

"Talitha Slagle."

"Welcome. My name's Vera."

"And if you want to know anything about these mountains, ask Vera," called a man from across the room. "She's lived here for a hundred years."

"Only ninety-four," boasted the woman. "And some of those I spent in Cincinnati, Ohio. Don't rush me, I'll get there."

Everyone in the class laughed.

"Talitha? How do you spell that?" asked Vera, anxious to learn more about the visitor.

As she spelled out the letters, Talitha was most impressed that here sat a woman who wanted so diligently to remember her name. That act alone made her feel most welcome.

Phill began the lesson with a prayer. Then he went directly into the lesson with the question, "What is driving your life"?

Talitha nearly choked on the juice she had been sipping.

"The focus of today's lesson is 'what aspects of your life are controlling you?' I hope you will leave this class with a renewed sense of purpose and direction. That you will be able to pinpoint the focus for your life, and that you will forget your own focus and follow God's planned focus for your life.

"As I was preparing for today's lesson, I felt like I was getting beaten up, that its words were slapping me upside the head."

Join the crowd! Talitha wanted to yell. She sat there spellbound, taking in every word, shocked that the same thoughts that had perplexed her lately were the very ones in this lesson. What shocked her even more was the realization that every person in this room was dealing with the same problem in their own lives.

Phill talked about how people were prone to get caught up in what they had, rather than who they were or what they did. "When we moved here, I had a new BMW. I sold it and bought a used pick-up truck."

Vera piped up. "A Carolina Cadillac. Why, I was twenty years old before I knew there was any other kind of vehicle!"

Everyone in the room again chuckled at her humor.

Talitha looked at the woman. She was well dressed, neatly groomed and looked fifteen to twenty years younger than her age. She had obviously, from her comments, traveled around the country and was very well read. *Stays on her toes.*

"Do you know why I sold my car?"

Class members had their own ideas, which they verbalized, but Phill answered, "I sold my BMW because no one would wave at me. Now when people pass the truck, they all throw up their hands and wave frantically."

Again, everyone in the room laughed.

Ah, mused Talitha with a sigh. *The simplicity of life.*

"People aren't only looking for the perfect life. They are searching for the perfect church."

"Huh! There ain't no such thing," voiced one of the men.

A woman, whom Talitha supposed to be his wife, spoke up with, "I had a cousin who once went to every church in a town, looking for the perfect one. She and her husband finally wound up at the first one they'd attended, realizing it wasn't so bad to start with."

Vera again offered her words of wisdom. "That's what you call Ecclesiastical Nomads."

At this, Talitha laughed aloud. She loved the intelligent ring of those words. Immediately, the gears in her head started turning as she pondered how she could write an article using them for a title.

"Some people call them church hoppers," Vera added, "but personally, I like the first expression better."

A sign of her intellect! Talitha liked this woman more all the time. She wondered if the woman seated next to her was the oldest woman, *next to Modena Brendle*, in Transylvania County. *A question I dare not ask her!*

Talitha made a note to ask Randy on her next visit to Kelly's. *He'll know, and if he doesn't, Doug will. Besides, that will give me an excuse to eat there one day this week.*

She turned her head to watch the expressions on each face, as she listened to them read passages from the lesson and make comments. Recently, she had felt a connection to her grandfather and her ancestors. Today, she felt a connection to this group of people circled around the room.

With one ear listening to the words of the lesson and one ear trying to hear and decipher her own thoughts, Talitha sought to see what changes should be made in her own life. *I wasn't unhappy with myself before I came here.* She looked at the people around the room. *And I'm not unhappy with myself now.*

But one reality hit Talitha, as bluntly as if she had been struck upside the head. *There's something missing in my life. There is more to living than getting up every morning, working every waking hour, maybe taking in a movie or dinner on the weekend, and going to bed.*

I'm going to find that "something else." And Cedar Mountain is just the place for me to do it!

Talitha heard a bell ringing outside the door. It was exactly like the old bell that had been rung to signal the end of class when she'd been a child in Sunday School. Phill quickly brought the lesson to a close while people closed their Bibles and grabbed their coats. She was reminded of how annoyed she became when, growing up, people would start pulling their hymnals from the racks when the minister began to wrap up his sermon, or put their sweaters and coats on during the final hymn.

If coffee is good to the last drop, why isn't the sermon or the hymn good to the last word? she'd ask as a child.

That same notion now crossed her mind. *Why aren't people in as big a rush to get to church as they are to get out of it?* She sneered to herself. *Another good article idea. This place is definitely a source of inspiration.*

Members of the class rushed to greet her. Ellyn introduced her to another woman who was relatively new to the area. "Why don't you sit together during church?"

"During church?" *Another one of my favorite expressions. If we are just now going into church, what have we been doing for the past hour?* As much as the expressions perturbed Talitha, they were exactly the same words she had heard while growing up around her own parents and grandparents.

Before Talitha had an opportunity to answer, the minister, who introduced himself as Alton Taylor grabbed her arm. "We're glad you decided to be a part of the family of Rocky Hill today. Would you play the organ for us this morning? You *can* play the organ, didn't Ellyn say?"

"Well . . . yes," she stumbled, "but it's been years . . . and what's the organist going to do?" Talitha had no intention of taking over someone else's act of service. She had learned long ago what an easy way that was to make enemies.

"She's going to direct the choir."

"Are you sure?"

"Absolutely. The pianist is not here today."

"Okay, but only if you're sure I won't be stepping on someone's toes in the process."

Talitha raised the cover on the organ and found the power button.

"Since you haven't played in a long time, why don't you go ahead and practice and that can be our prelude?" Preacher Taylor suggested.

Talitha jeered. These people were so gracious and appreciative of the gift of music that they probably wouldn't have minded had she practiced for a few minutes. She put her coat and grandfather's Bible down on the front pew behind the organ, scooted the bench to a comfortable position and removed her heels.

Lucky for me my organ teacher can't see me playing barefoot. I'd hear her screaming from here. She pushed the stops for her desired registration. *And lucky for me that she made me practice over and over on the same pieces until they were permanently etched in my memory.* Thoughts of her grandfather crossed her mind as she wondered whether she would have spent so much time practicing had he not been such an advocate of music. *Especially church music.*

Talitha began to play Bach's *Jesu, Joy of Man's Desiring,* hoping it would be recognized by the listeners. Then she wondered whether anyone was listening, or if she was merely playing "music to talk by," another of her pet peeves from childhood.

An elderly woman, supported by a younger woman, entered the side door and stepped up to the organ. "Are you the woman who played down the street a few weeks ago."

"I did play at Blue Ridge Baptist, if that's what you mean," explained Talitha.

"You're a writer?"

"Yes."

"My best friend came home and you were all she could talk about for days. You were so good," according to her, "that you inspired me. I'm playing today. My own arrangement of *All Hail the Power.*"

The woman holding onto the elderly woman leaned over to Talitha. "My mother was a classically trained concert pianist. She's 89 years old, and this is a tremendous event for her. Thank you for getting her to do this again."

As the choir marched in from the back and took their seats in the loft behind the pulpit, the mother and daughter couple found a pew.

Alton took his place and asked, "Who's had a prayer answered this week?"

Talitha raised her hand proudly, at the same time hoping that her present prayer, of not having to tell what that request had been - that her beloved Carolina Panthers would win the ball game the preceding week – would not be discovered.

When it came time for the offertory, the concert pianist slowly approached the piano. Although it was apparent her step had slowed significantly, it was equally apparent that the zip in her eyes and the twinkle in her imp-like spirit had not. Her fingers were all over the piano keys, dusting out any cobwebs that might have accumulated during the past several years. Talitha stared at the woman in amazement, while wondering if she would ever be able to play that well. *Especially at 89! I'll be lucky to play Tiddly Winks, much less the piano!*

The minute the service was over, Talitha rushed from the organ to the woman who had played the piano.

"Oh, you're just wonderful!" the woman said, grabbing Talitha's hand.

"No, *you* are the one who's wonderful. I'd give anything just to still be kicking at your age, much less play the piano like that!" Having heard the minister announce the woman's name as Lucille Dahl, Talitha continued, "Your name suits you perfectly. You truly *are* a 'doll.'"

The two women clutched each others' hands for several seconds while everyone else waited to speak to them. There was a rhythm that passed through them, an artistic understanding and appreciation that was difficult for the rest of the congregation to sense, but something that stirred Talitha's soul in a way it had never been moved before.

Suddenly there was something on her mind besides the Panthers and now, even though she intended to enjoy every play of the game and cheer for her home team, she knew that, no matter what the outcome of the game, there would be some mind-bending questions going on in the back of her mind.

Talitha headed for her car, but was stopped by a man she recognized from the Sunday School class.

"Here, I want you to have this." He handed her a gold coin.

"Thank you." Talitha was surprised at his kind act. "Do you treat all the visitors this way?"

"No." The man gave her a huge grin. "But I understand you know my son, Whitson Lambert. He gave me eighty gold coins recently in honor of my eightieth birthday, and I felt the urge to share one with you."

"Whitson's your son?"

"He sure is."

"Then you must be kin to the Heath's."

"Sure am, on my wife's side."

What a small world it is.

"Yes, it is a small world, Talitha., and you can't escape me. I'm everywhere."

Carolina's Cardiac Cats diminished farther into the background as this woman finally listened to the voice and began to weigh her life, her past and her future.

When it came time for the afternoon game, Talitha had to pull herself away from Pretty Place, the nearby chapel down Solomon Jones Road that opened onto a panoramic view of miles and miles of mountains and valleys. She'd gone straight there from church and sat reading her Bible and asking questions of "the Voice" that had been following, or *leading*, her lately.

With the overtime touchdown that won the Panthers the game, Talitha felt like there had been not one, but two wins that day.

And both of them took a little extra time.

Chapter 14

Talitha got up and put on her robe, a luxury she rarely enjoyed while working for the newspaper. She went to the kitchen and turned on the coffeemaker, then to the front window and pulled up the blinds. There was a light mist enveloping the branches of the trees in the front yard that gave the entire area a mystical appearance.

This was the morning she'd been planning for a long time, the morning she'd intended to have yesterday when God obviously had other plans for her.

She heard the coffeemaker stop dripping and moved back

to the kitchen to get a mug of fresh "wake-up juice," as Calvin had referred to it. As she turned to walk back into the den to sit in one of the wing chairs, she noticed a red glow on the trees.

The fog must be lifting. She fell back into the chair and crossed her legs while sipping slowly on the coffee and getting into a relaxing mode for the rest of the day. Talitha closed her eyes for a few seconds and thought about her grandfather and how much fun they could have had in this place together. When she opened her eyes, she noticed that the fog had again dropped over the surroundings. *Guess it can't make up its mind.*

She sipped a little more "wake-up juice" from the coffee cup and went back to her thoughts of her grandfather. He would have been so proud that she had followed her dream, and that she was settling in a place that held so many memories of things she had treasured as a child.

A growling from her stomach told her that it was time to find something to eat this morning. She put on some eggs to boil, holding to her resolution of losing some weight for the New Year. *Mine and how many other people's?* she questioned herself.

When she stepped back into the den, she noticed that the trees outside were again giving off a reddish glow. Talitha had had enough of the games with Mother Nature. She walked over to the front window and looked outside, trying to decide what was going on with the sun and the fog.

What she saw was a half-moon shell over the trees, right in her view from the window, that appeared to be holding off the fog. All the rest of the area was covered by a light, transparent mist, hovering over the trees like a sheer blanket.

There really is something magical about this place.

During the course of the evening, the temperature had dropped drastically, setting the record for the coldest night in March that Cedar Mountain had seen in over a century. Even so, after breakfast, Talitha bravely ventured out onto the screened porch, her mug of Hazelnut Vanilla coffee clasped between her hands as her only defense against the cold, as she took a good look at the pond in front of the cabin. From this viewpoint, she gathered that the pond was much larger than she had thought from the road, and that there was a waterfall at the back corner of it. *Something I'll have to check out when it's a bit warmer!* To the left was a picnic table, which she had noticed the first time she spotted the cabin; to the right was a long stone bench, standing near the water's edge with a perfect vantage point of the waterfall. There was an island in the lake that couldn't be seen from the road.

A perfect spot to decorate for Christmas! She imagined a tree reflecting its lights in the middle of the pond. Talitha closed her eyes for a second and pretended to see such a tree with her grandfather. When she opened them, there seemed to be tiny lights flickering, like stars twinkling all over the water.

By the time she had reached for her pad and pen, the stars were gone. *In the twinkling of an eye. What's that song my grandmother used to sing with that phrase?* Her mind began a mental search, trying to remember the last time she'd heard that phrase. *Why does it stand out so distinctly in my mind?*

Talitha looked all around the house for a hymnbook. Ellyn had attended to every possible need and detail to make this a perfect location for a vacation. *Or writer's retreat. She's a musician. There has to be a hymnbook in here somewhere.*

Not wanting to look through drawers that weren't hers,

she jumped in her car and raced to the end of Reasonover Road, turning into the church parking lot at Blue Ridge Baptist. *Oh, please let there be someone here,* she begged. There were no cars in the parking lot. *Should I try the door?* Talitha started to turn around and head back to Rocky Hill.

Why not? she thought. *Check the door.* Talitha turned off her car and walked up the ramp.

I'm wasting my time. By the time I find a hymnbook, I'm going to forget why I wanted it in the first place. She turned the doorknob. *Just as I figured.* It wouldn't turn. She walked around to the back of the sanctuary.

"Hey, Talitha! Something I can help you with today?"

Talitha looked up to see Raymond doing yard work on the other side of the church. *Is he the appointed groundskeeper? He's here every time I have a need.* She couldn't help but think about Jesus at the tomb as the gardener in the Resurrection story. Here were several tombs and here was a gardener.

"I can't believe my luck! I need a hymnbook to look up a specific song and I don't have one with me."

Raymond unlocked the crimson door for her and when Talitha reached onto the back pew for a hymnal, she saw a small white Bible in the rack. *That looks exactly like the one my grandparents gave me when I was in the second grade.* They had even bought if from her for a school fundraiser. It was white leather and had a brass zipper around the outer three edges of pages.

She suddenly realized the irony in that. *A school fundraiser? Why, they won't hardly let kids pray in school nowadays, much less have a Bible.* She thought about the fact that the Bible was taught for a week in literature classes, but it could not be taught in classes that bore any resemblance to a religious nature.

Talitha thought back to the Bible fundraiser. Not only had the school sold various styles of the King James' version of the Holy Bible, they had sold bookmarks that bore the Ten Commandments or the Golden Rule. And they had sold cross necklaces and bracelets with Bible charms on them.

How wonderful that I got that Biblical training as a young child. Otherwise, I'd probably have no recollection of it now. She smiled as she thought of all the items her grandfather had bought from her for that project. *Something for every person in the family for Christmas.*

"Talitha?" Raymond was glaring at her with a quizzical look on his face.

She had no idea how many times he had called her name or how long she had been standing there for she was so completely wrapped up in thinking about how schools used to make money off everyone's love for religiously-inspired gifts.

"Sorry. My mind was back in the second grade. I was thinking about my first Bible. My grandparents gave it to me that year." Talitha didn't bother to tell him she had no idea where it was now, or how long it had been since she had opened its pages.

"It must have been wonderful to grow up in a family like that. We didn't go to church in my family. In fact, my wife came for years by herself. I got my first Bible three years ago. That's when I found salvation and joined the church." Raymond walked down the aisle to the front pew. "I've got it here. I brought it with me this morning so I could read God's word in His house. There's no difference, I know. But it's just something I like to do."

"I didn't think anyone was here when I saw no cars in the parking lot."

"My wife dropped me off on her way into town. I had the day off and decided to make sure the church yard was all ready for spring. Figured I'd weed out the beds where all the day lilies come up. Hmmph," he sighed, "it's a funny thing. No one ever planted them, but there's a whole row of them along the front of the church that come up every summer. Then we've got a butterfly bush over there in that corner. Sometimes when we open the church windows, the butterflies will fly right in the sanctuary."

He got a big grin on his face. "My little granddaughter asked me one time if they were angels."

Raymond reached down and picked up a Bible off the front pew. The corners were badly bent and the pages appeared to have been turned back and forth like an old phone directory.

And he's only used this thing three years? He must be pretty rough on it. She looked up at Raymond to see the face of a Godly man. *Or use it a lot.*

Talitha was reminded that she had to struggle to remember the order of the books and find the simplest verses in the Bible.

"Is there something in particular you're lookin' for?" he asked, seeing her confusion.

"There was." She looked down again at the worn pages of his Bible. "But I think I've already found it, in the twinkling of an eye, when I wasn't even looking for it."

Chapter 15

Talitha walked into Kelly's just in time to see Preacher, Buster and Joan getting up from their table.

"Welcome back," greeted Preacher, giving her a huge hug. "I hear you're here to get some writing done this week."

"That's right, if I don't freeze to death first," she laughed. "I hear Buster went to Las Vegas for a bowling tournament," Talitha said to Joan.

"Reno," she corrected.

"How'd he do?"

Buster wheeled around. "See that big trophy back there

beside Mickey's walking cane? That's how I did!"

"Wow!" Talitha walked back to see the plaque of writing on the trophy. "Third place?" She turned to Buster. "Out of bowlers from all over the country, you mean you really truly won third place?"

While Buster nodded his head with a big grin on his face, Preacher called out, "Don't let him kid you. He bought that off some guy on the street and brought it home with him."

"I thought preachers weren't supposed to lie!" Buster defended.

"They're not," laughed Preacher. "But a gentle pull on a person's leg never hurt anybody."

"That was more than a 'gentle' pull of the leg. That was a low blow."

Talitha laughed aloud. "So this is my welcome to Cedar Mountain?"

"Hey," yelled Miss B coming around the corner with a large tray covered with plates of food, "why should today be any different?"

Doug joined the small group that had gathered around the trophy. "Pretty nice, isn't it?" he asked. Then he gave Talitha a hug. "I didn't get to speak when you came in the door, there was such a long line."

"This trophy's so fine that I believe I feel a new story coming on," Talitha announced.

"About my trophy?" asked Buster.

"More like about everyone's reaction to the trophy."

"Huh?"

"This is the kind of place people want to come. On their

lunch break, on their free days and weekends, on their vacations. Do you have any idea how many people would give their right arm to leave the stress and schedules of a huge downtown office and come here, even if only for a day's getaway?"

She listed all the terrific attributes that would attract people to this place.

"Maybe I'd better forego lunch and write a travel article about this place."

"Do you really think people would want to come here and see us?" asked Charlie.

"See you, hear you and eat the food," she replied. "Besides," she added, "I don't see any of you going any place else."

"I like this gal better all the time," declared Buster.

"When are you moving here permanently?" Joan asked.

"Just as soon as I can find a place to live."

"Then you'd better get over here and eat," ordered Regina, who had walked in the door and heard all the commotion. She grabbed a place mat and a menu and cleaned off a table for the guest. "My Uncle Burrell is coming in shortly and he's got a house that will soon be ready to rent."

"Burrell? Didn't I meet him at the church Sunday?"

"You sure did. His wife, Flora, was there, too."

"That's good," agreed Doug. "If you move into Burrell's house, you'll be my neighbor."

"Really?" asked Talitha. "This deal is sounding more intriguing by the minute."

"So you'll be ready for all of us to show up for dinner tomorrow night?" Regina asked.

"Yeah, sure, if Kelly's is catering."

"We can do it," Randy stated, coming out of the kitchen to give Talitha a hug. "I thought I heard you out here. How's the writing coming?"

"It's coming. I love being in the Masterson's cabin. That place is full of inspiration."

I truly am at home here, she sensed. *All because of a restaurant, a small, white wooden church and a grandfather who loved me very much.* In that instant, Talitha knew that God was working out all the details for her to move to Cedar Mountain. She could feel it inside, just like Preacher and Alton had talked about. Just like Whitson Lambert had talked about. *And just like the preacher when I was a little girl talked about.*

"God will take care of you."

She wondered if the words she heard were a memory of her grandmother singing that old hymn or the same voice that had been guiding her, as of late.

The lunch with Burrell proved to be most productive. By the time he said good-bye, Talitha had an appointment for that evening to see his rental house. But from the gut feeling she already sensed, sight unseen, that she would soon be the newest resident on Reasonover Road.

Once the crowd slowed down, Randy stopped to visit a few minutes at Talitha's table while she finished taking notes about the rental house, Buster's trophy and all the tourist attractions in Transylvania County. "So how soon are you moving? Hope and I can help you."

"Good, then I can have the two of you over to my house for dinner."

"You just come to our house. We have to cook anyway. Then you can keep on writing."

"I sure can't ask for more than that."

"You do know that cabin you're staying in this week is where Percy lived, don't you?"

"No, I don't. Or at least, I didn't until just now."

"Uh-huh. He and his two sisters lived in that house."

"How long ago was that?"

"I'm not sure, but it was a long time ago."

Doug walked by and heard the question. "It was back in the forties, when I was a boy. That was where we rounded the curve and the car slid off in the snow. Percy walked out to the road, reached under the bumper, picked the car up and set it back on the road. I've never seen anybody that strong in my life. I'd always thought my Uncle Paul was the strongest man on the mountain, but I found out different that day."

Talitha had heard about Percy before she ever saw Cedar

Mountain. He, like Modena, was a legend among the old-timers.

"I can't believe he'd go out in the cold and break the ice off the pump and take a bath in that freezing cold water."

"Well, he did. Thought it had some healing powers in it to bathe in the water when it was that cold. I don't know if he ever took a bath in the summer, but he sure wore that pump out in the winter."

Shivers ran up Talitha's spine at the thought. "As cold as was this morning, he'd have loved the water."

The thought of Percy in the ice cold water brought to mind many of the stories that Randy and Doug had told her prior to her visit to Cedar Mountain. After going back to the church this morning for the hymnbook, there was one other question still roaming in Talitha's head.

I think a trip to see Modena Brendle is in order.

"Hey, Randy, can I get two orders of vegetable soup to go? Then I've got to get out of here. I have some research to take care of this afternoon."

"Sure thing."

It wasn't long before Talitha was on her way to Reasonover Road. *And some answers.*

"Thank ya kindly for the soup. Randy's good t' keep a check on me on the real cold days. We had one lady freeze t' death up here during a blizzard. Gets so bad up here some winters that they have t' airlift people out."

Talitha got more answers than she had questions. Modena had decided she wanted to be a celebrity and she was more than happy to give the writer all the details she needed.

"I've got one last question, Modena. When I went to the church at Rocky Hill the other Sunday, someone said,"

"I know wha'chur a-gonna ask. Heaven's no, that church t'weren't built from one tree. Why, that legendary big old poplar tree! Ever' one in the county's laid claim to that tree. That was somebody's mighty tall tale."

Modena leaned over her new brass spittoon that Talitha brought her. "But don'chu go telling anybody I said so. I don't wanna be busting nobody's bubble."

Ping! Modena was a perfect shot with the tobacco juice.

Chapter 16

When Talitha got to the point in the curve where she could see the front yard of her "stepping stone," as she called her small cottage, she could see Mrs. Pope, Flora, in the yard planting flowers in front of the white picket fence. *What a fitting name for her.* She turned into the drive and heard a dog barking as it came to greet her, wagging its tail and jumping up to say, "Hello."

Burrell Pope came briskly walking from his house next door. "Welcome home. Randy, Michael and Regina are coming over later to bring supper."

"How'd they know I was here?"

"Honey, you're in Cedar Mountain now, where everyone knows whose check is good and whose husband is not!"

"Guess that means I have to be on my best behavior, huh?"

Burrell smiled. "Talitha, it's evident to watch you that you're always on your best behavior."

"Thanks, but no one's *always* on their best behavior. But I'll remember you said that, anyway."

The thought of walking inside the front door of a place already furnished, complete with linens, dishes and every household commodity she could possibly need, caused the newcomer to want to jump up and down like the dog.

Flora took off her gardening gloves and gave Talitha a bear hug. "I'm so glad you're here. I could hardly wait until you got here."

"The key's already in the door waiting for you." Burrell also gave her a hug. "Come on inside and see how we've got it fixed up for you."

Talitha knew she was in for a treat before she walked into the house. There was a huge assortment of pink and white balloons tied to the floor lamp beside the leather recliner. A large arrangement of freshly cut pale-pink peonies and orange-colored wild honeysuckle were in a vase on the coffee table of the den. The television was turned to a lovely classical music station, letting the notes fill the air and be swirled around by the ceiling fan's blades. Even the air conditioner had cooled the house to a comfortable temperature.

She walked back outside, feeling right at home.

"How do you like it?" called Flora.

"It's heavenly. Absolutely heavenly. From the flowers to

the music to the pieces of art hanging on the walls. And I especially love the faux paint job on the den wall with the border of wild strawberries, morning glories, bunnies and birds. I'll feel like I'm outdoors on a spring morning even when it's the dead of winter."

"I hope it will inspire you. I've tried to choose colors and plants that I thought you'd like."

"It couldn't be more beautiful. If I can't write in this surrounding, I might as well pack up and go home."

"You are home," Burrell stated firmly as he turned and walked back toward his house.

"You are home," came the voice firmly.

Talitha thought fondly of the mountain retreat her grandparents had once bought. And how they gave it to the family who lived in it for years and tended it. That selfless gift had manifested itself in another generation, given back to a descendant. Burrell and Flora had now gone out of their way to give her a good home. She recalled a scripture about how the sins of the father carried over for generations. Sighing heavily, she whispered, "I'm not sure about the sins of the father, but I certainly do know about the gifts of the father." *And the Father.*

She spoke to the mountain that sat directly behind her back porch, "I am home, Granddaddy. Thank you."

Chapter 17

The third day? What is it that sticks out in my head about the third day?

And the worst day after surgery is usually the third day, according to an article I once wrote.

Whatever it was, Talitha was exhausted. She had two articles that needed to be drafted, another that needed to be proofed, and she was so tired from the day of unpacking that she could barely move when she passed the last fast food joint before making the drive up the mountain.

That's a first. I don't know that I've ever been too tired to eat.

Talitha decided an hour's nap would be the best solution before she tried to do anything else, whether that be to eat, write or unpack. However, when she drove into her driveway and saw Miss Kitty, the Pope's cat that had already taken up residence by sitting on her front porch, what she saw was a dwelling that looked "lived in" – a dwelling that looked like she already belonged. That was enough to convince her to leave the rest of the unloading until the next day, hoping to be able to get into some vague sense of writing mode, and then take a restful shower and finish reading the bi-weekly newspaper in the plush leather recliner.

When she got out of the car, her body suddenly was raring to go, feeling a complete renewal of spirit, energy and thought. Having no patio furniture yet moved, she reached in her pantry and grabbed the one beach chair she had thrown in there earlier while she had been pulling things from the trunk. Talitha quickly pulled it from its canvas case, unfolded it and set it on the front porch, finding a spot where she could get the best view of her "very own" yard.

She grabbed her laptop and a soda from the fridge – one of the few things in it since she had not yet visited the grocery store. *Like I need any more energy!* she mused, noticing it was the "leaded" version.

Talitha took a small sip of the drink, set in on the porch beside her and began to type. Before she knew it, she had completed three articles and begun a whimsical non-fiction book that had squiggled like a worm through her thoughts during the day of moving and unpacking.

When she realized how much and swiftly her work was pouring out, she stopped and looked around her. It was then that she sensed that her heart was pumping like it did when she had swum laps, taken mile jogs or been to aerobics class.

What is it about this place? She recalled the week she had stayed at the red cabin on the small lake. *Is there really, truly a magic to Cedar Mountain?* Talitha sat her laptop in the chair and took a thorough tour of the house, in the front and the back, then on both sides, trying to take in as many details as possible.

No wonder Jesus went to the mountain or the lake to get rejuvenated. Talitha realized that she didn't remember ever having this much energy or brainpower before, and especially after a day of climbing, moving and hauling boxes for hours. *No wonder Jesus . . . Jesus . . . that's it.*

On the third day, he arose from the grave so that we could have eternal life.

A smile, larger than she'd ever had when she'd cracked a case open with an investigative theory, spread across Talitha's face. *No wonder I have all this energy. Eternal life, huh? And on the third day, huh?*

The newcomer noticed the water of the creek and the mountains that surrounded her, and the calm serenity fashioned by the straight and willowy evergreen trees.

Perhaps there truly is a magic and a charm about this place. But I think it goes a lot deeper than just the air here. And I think the word starts with a "J."

What had snapped her into this instantaneous productive spell? *Was it Miss Kitty sitting on the porch to welcome me home? Was it all the birds singing beautiful rills from the treetops? Was it all the lush greenery of spring? Was it the refreshing shower that had just swept through, leaving all the streets and leaves and blades* of grass looking clean and vibrant? Was it the cloudless blue sky that followed the dark gray storm clouds? Was it the strength of all the boulders in the front yard, cascading down the hill from the roadside? Was it the sound of the rippling water in the creek behind the house? Was it the view of a mountain in front of her house, and another in back of her house? Was it . . .

Or is it all of the above? she asked herself, taking a walk all the way around the outside perimeters of the house again.

She happened to notice a wooden planter on the ground where Flora had placed four small flowerpots the day she first arrived, each one with a different flowering plant. On it she saw a ladybug walking around the top edges, inspecting the whole thing. *My Lady Luck,* she smiled.

I know, it's my lucky place to be.

"Or blessed," came the words from nowhere. Talitha wheeled around to make sure that Flora wasn't talking to her. A quick inspection indicated that she was alone. *Where do those words keep coming from?*

She moved back to her chair on the porch and picked up her notes, determined to put some sort of finish on one of the three articles.

"Have you had dinner?" This time there was definitely someone speaking to her.

Talitha heard Flora's voice through the bushes. It wasn't but a minute until she heard footsteps in the gravel driveway. "No, not exactly."

What a dumb answer for a word person to give for such a simple question.

"It's Prime Rib night at Grammy's," Burrell called, pulling

the car up the driveway. "Why don't you come join us?"

"I couldn't possibly," answered Talitha. She had seen the huge sign prominently hung from the side of the one Cedar Mountain restaurant declaring that reservations were required. "They won't be expecting me."

"That doesn't matter. Hop in." Burrell got out and opened the back door of the car for his new neighbor.

She didn't have the heart to tell him that she wasn't nearly ready to go anywhere.

"I'm sure they've got plenty," he assured, pulling out of the driveway and onto the curvy road.

Talitha snickered. *I can just see me going into a restaurant on a Friday night at home with no reservation and have any hope of getting seated, much less being served the Prime Rib special.* She admired the scenery as Burrell whipped around the curves that had been home to him for nearly seventy years. *Surely I can order a burger or something; I can't see Prime Rib being the meal of choice here on the side of some mountain. It would probably taste like shoe leather anyway.*

In less than five minutes, they were parked and inside the restaurant.

"Got room for one more?" Burrell asked the waitress who obviously knew him.

"Let me check." She made a quick jaunt to the kitchen and was right back. "No problem."

Burrell smiled warmly across the table. "See? I told you they'd be plenty."

So much for the security of a no-fail burger. Guess it's shoe leather tonight.

Before Talitha had a chance to form an opinion of the

eating establishment, the waitress was back with her water and salad. Not quite the same as the service in the big city, she sighed, wondering how many hours of her life had been spent waiting on salads and food orders.

It wasn't long before the guest was glad she had accepted the invitation to come. *But then it wasn't really an invitation – it was more like an order.* She smiled as she listened to the stories Burrell was sharing with her. *Thank goodness, I didn't object.* Her ears were hearing the man's voice, but her mind was chiding her for what she almost gave up simply because of her preconceived notions.

"Here's our food," announced Flora.

Talitha turned her head. *Surely not already.* But the waitress balanced a tray that held all three of their plates. As she set each person's prime rib, done to individually ordered perfection, Talitha noticed that the cuts of beef resembled nothing like shoe leather.

Looks like all my preconceived notions are going down the tube.

She hurriedly bit into the entrée only to find that it was the most delicious slice of prime rib she'd ever eaten. *Not to mention this baked potato,* she mused, glaring in disbelief at the largest potato she'd ever seen on a plate. *And it, too, is done to perfection. Not like all those I normally get that are only about half-done.*

Talitha glanced around the room. All of the plates within sight looked equally as filled to the brim and the guests all seemed to have a smile on their faces. *Both from the food and the atmosphere, I assume.*

By the time the waitress came back to check on dessert orders, there were no takers. Both Talitha and Flora asked for a box, while Burrell wrapped his leftovers in a piece of foil for his dog.

The real reason for "doggie" bags. How long has it been since I actually saw someone taking food home for their pet?

"Would you like to see the nicest house in Cedar Mountain?" Burrell asked as he started the car.

"Well, maybe some other,"

"It won't take but a minute."

As Burrell turned the car up the private road, Talitha noticed the sign that specifically stated, "No Visitors."

"Are you sure it's okay for us to be here?" she asked, having visions of hearing shotgun fire and ducking in the back seat.

Burrell laughed. "I come up here all the time."

"Anytime there's a problem that warrants a handyman, Burrell's called," explained Flora.

"Oh," nodded Talitha, breathing a bit easier until she got a glimpse of the steep drop down the mountain beside the narrow road they were traveling. Then she realized that Burrell had been right when he'd stated that it would only take a minute for their journey. They were going faster than she remembered driving down the freeway.

Suddenly the car came to an abrupt halt. "Hi," greeted Burrell, seeing a couple with their children sitting out in the yard, enjoying the cool of the early evening and roasting marshmallows in the chimineas.

"Hi, Todd. We have a new neighbor. Mind if we take her up and show her Gene's house?"

"Not a bit," came the friendly answer. "I'll grab the four-wheeler and be up right behind you."

"We won't stay but a minute," promised Flora. "I know you're terribly busy."

"Yes, I really," Her sentence stopped in midstream as she looked at the huge complex of a home that sprawled out in front of her.

It sat on the crest of the mountain's peak and had perfect views of what Burrell described as "twelve miles. You can even see the radio towers two cities over."

While Todd shook hands and caught up on the recent happenings with Burrell and Flora, Talitha gazed at the breathtakingly beautiful view out in front of her, ignoring everything and everybody but the majesty that heralded from being atop this mountain.

"Talitha, this is Todd. This house is his family's home place."

She forced herself to look away from the sunset and nod to the man facing her. "Pleased to meet you. It's most gracious of you to allow us to come here."

"Any friend of Burrell's is a friend of mine. He and my dad go way back. If there was anything we couldn't take care of, we always called on Burrell."

Talitha grinned in understanding. "Is there anything he can't do?"

"Not to hear any of you tell it," Flora chuckled.

"Would you like to see inside the house?" Burrell asked.

"Maybe in a minute. If you don't mind, I'd love just to watch this sky for a little longer. I don't know that I've ever seen a more radiant sunset."

"They were always like that up here," Todd admitted. "The really neat thing about this house is the fact that you can see the sunrise and the sunset. There are no trees in the way to block the view."

Talitha gazed at the sprawling land around her. Todd was right. The house was actually up taller than the treetops. She had seen many places in the mountains with her grandparents before, but none that compared to the one where she stood. It was indeed a mansion, as fine a home as any she'd seen in the most glamorous and prestigious sections of Charlotte.

The interior was even more magnificent that the exterior. Vaulted ceilings and large windows that lined the walls gave way to a brightness that was unusual for most of the mountain homes. An oversized fireplace, which opened to both sides, stood in the middle of a large open room that served as a living room, dining area and kitchen. The entire hearth and fireplace were made from massive stones that went clear up to the high ceiling, and past for the chimney. There was no view of the surrounding mountains that wasn't visible from the strategically placed windows – windows that were as large as entire walls in most average-sized homes.

"You should hear Talitha play. She's quite a musician," bragged Burrell.

"Is that so?" Todd asked. "Why don't you follow me downstairs? There's something there I think you'd like to see."

Sure enough, there was a Gulbransen theater organ placed in a perfect niche in front of the window on the bottom level of the house that overlooked at least one whole county.

Talitha remembered the style of instrument well. It was just like the one she had taken lessons on as a teenager. It was the one that had the brightly colored tabs with the glossy pearl finish. It was just like the one her teacher had at home, the one that had all the fun doo-dads on it back in the day before synthesizers and Moog machines.

"Can you do anything with this?" Burrell teased.

"Can I!" Talitha retorted, glancing back over her shoulder at Todd, who had been followed by his wife and children. She waited for some sign of approval before she sat down at the instrument.

"Have at it," were the only words she needed to hear before plopping herself on the bench and finding that exact spot to feel the pedals perfectly balanced underneath her feet.

By the time they had all made some remark about the last time the instrument had been touched and predictions about whether it would even still play, Talitha had pushed a few tabs and buttons and was ripping out tune after tune that her teacher had taught her to show off this particular style of organ.

"Doesn't sound like there's anything wrong with it to me," Burrell observed.

"I didn't know it still had that in it," Todd confessed. His eyes denoted the same look of surprise as did those of his wife and children.

After several minutes of a non-stop concert, enhanced by the masterfully orchestrated change of stops during and between solos, Talitha stopped and rubbed her fingers across the tops of the keys, much like a man running his fingers over the smooth finish of a hotrod.

"Just like being in a cockpit," she laughed, basking in the memories evoked by the electronic instrument.

"Would you like to have it?" asked Todd.

Talitha looked at him in disbelief. "Oh, I'd love to have it, but there's no way I could afford it right now." It wasn't until after she'd made the statement that she remembered how much money was actually in her bank account. She'd made such a point of not spending anymore than she had when she worked at the newspaper that she'd literally put the inheritance out of her mind.

"I'll bet he'd work out some sort of payment arrangement with you," suggested Burrell.

"Oh, no," replied Todd. "I don't want your money. I asked if you'd like to have it."

The stunned woman's eyes were full of shock.

"It hasn't sounded like that in years." He paused. "Actually, ever. And I'd love for you to have it. It would be much better getting used and being appreciated than sitting here collecting dust."

Talitha's eyes were still staring at Todd and her jaws were trying to make some sort of motion so that she could respond to his generous offer. "I . . . I'd be . . . I'd be pleased to have it. But I couldn't possibly take it."

"And why not?" admonished Todd. "I offered it to you. I wouldn't have offered if I didn't want you to have it."

She managed a slight smile. "Then thank you. I'd love to have it." Talitha rubbed her fingers across the keys again.

"Good. Then it's settled," proclaimed Todd. "I'll even have a couple of my men load it on the big truck this week and I'll bring it to you."

"You can't beat that," stated Burrell, lending a hand to Talitha as she spun around to get off the bench.

"I don't know what to say," she said to Flora.

"Say thank you."

"C'mon, let's get back outside," called one of the kids. "I want to make some s'mores."

Talitha apologized, fearful that she'd taken up too much of their family time.

"Don't even mention it," offered Todd's wife. "That was the highlight of the evening."

"I'd never even heard the organ played," admitted one of the daughters.

The three guests followed the four-wheeler, the children and the family dog halfway back down the mountain and said their good-byes after fixing a s'more each to keep the children happy.

Talitha sat with her head laid against the back of the seat as they coasted down the steep road, much slower than they'd ascended it. Never did she recall having a better meal or having more fun than she had this evening.

She was in such a trance that she'd completely forgotten about any writing projects until she was unlocking her front door.

"It's on me the next time," she called to Burrell and Flora as they walked toward their front door.

"Just play me some more of that pretty music," Burrell replied. "That's good enough for me."

"You got it." The words echoed across the lawn as Talitha rushed inside to her computer, full of ideas for new stories.

Chapter 18

On Saturday, Talitha remembered she had still not gone to the grocery store. She decided a stop at Grammy's would be quicker than running all the way to Brevard. *Especially when I want to go to my first concert there tonight.* She made a quick list of all the things that she needed and the several errands that demanded her attention for when she was off the mountain.

This business of making one big trip instead of twenty small ones is going to save me a bundle of time. I should be able to get out two extra articles a week just from that.

By the time Talitha arrived at the restaurant, she'd made a

list of ways she could save time, even with the drive into town taking longer. She'd read about a new hardware store and a gift shop opening at the corner in Cedar Mountain. They had cards in the Welcome Center. *What more could I want?*

As she entered Grammy's, given that the only thing she'd eaten there was prime rib the previous evening, it dawned on her that she'd never seen a menu and she didn't have her reading glasses. *Guess I'll go for the no-fail burger this time.*

There was a familiar face on the man seated next to her table. "Say, aren't you," she began.

Before she had a chance to finish her inquiry, the man had stopped her in mid-sentence. "The owner of the hardware."

"Yes, Mack, isn't it? I recognized you from that article in the newspaper."

He gave a half smile. "Everybody in Transylvania County must have read that article. People have been coming by the store all week and I wasn't even there. I was in Florida."

Talitha watched as he dipped chicken strips in honey mustard and French fries in ketchup.

"You by yourself?" he asked.

"Yes, I'm new here."

"I already knew that. Why don't you join me?"

Talitha thanked Mack and accepted his invitation. "How'd you know I was new?"

"I grew up here. Know everybody in Cedar Mountain. Moved away for a while, but there's no place like here."

"You're right about that."

"So what are you doing here?"

"Just checking out the place. I'm a writer and it looked like a good place to be."

"Nice and quiet, all right. What kind of writer?"

"I was an investigative reporter for several years, seventeen to be exact, with the *Monroe Enquirer-Journal*.

"You're kidding! When I moved away for a while, that's only twenty miles from where I lived. Now you know why I'm back here."

Talitha snickered. "Yes, you do have a point."

"So you going to tell me your name or are you going to continue to be a stranger?"

"I'm sorry, I didn't mean to be rude."

"You weren't rude. I wouldn't have let you join me if you were rude."

Talitha smiled again. There was a charming dry wit about the man seated across from her. He reminded her slightly of Calvin. "The name's Talitha. Talitha Slagle."

"Pleased to meet you Talitha. Why don't you come down to the store and have a look around?"

"I'd love to."

"I've got to be running now, but I'll see you when you finish eating." Mack picked up both tickets.

Talitha reached for hers. "You don't have to do that. I had no intention of you paying for mine."

He pulled his hand away. "I'm from the old school. We don't allow women to pay."

Before she had a chance to respond, Burrell came in the door. "Hey, what are you doing with him?"

Mack turned around and yelled a loud hello.

Talitha laughed. So far she knew everyone she had seen in

Cedar Mountain. At this rate, she'd know the entire population by the end of the week.

Burrell took a seat where Mack had been. "Don't mind if I join you, do you?"

"I could never mind if you joined me. But you'd better be careful," she warned. "The last time you came in a restaurant and sat down with me, you wound up getting me for a neighbor!"

The kindly man laughed. "Lucky, wasn't I?"

"I'm the one who was lucky."

The waitress showed up to take his order. It was obvious by her conversation with Burrell that he was a regular.

"You must come here a lot."

"Everyday."

"What about Flora?"

"I usually take her something. Say, if you're busy writing, why don't you let me bring you something back? Then you can keep working."

"Thanks. That's a most kind offer and I may take you up on it some days. But most of the time, I'm ready for a break by lunch. In the summers, I get up early and try to have all my day's writing done by ten o'clock. In the winter, I'm rarely up before ten o'clock."

"That's some schedule. What do you do the rest of the time?"

"Either interview people or scan the area for other stories of interest."

"There's plenty of them around here."

Talitha smiled and nodded. "I'm finding that out."

As the reporter leaned back in her chair and looked around

the place, with its paying customers – as many visitors as local residents – and it employees – most of whom had grown up in the area – she saw the reason for the stories. The place where she'd grown up was full of stories. The place she'd lived and worked for the past seventeen years was full of stories. It struck her, now, that every place in the world was a rich field, fertile with stories. The thing that was different about Cedar Mountain, and other places squirreled away back in the hills, was that people viewed life differently. They had a deeper appreciation for it. So far, it seemed that everyone she'd met from Cedar Mountain had either left and then moved back, unable or unwilling to let go of that natural, relaxing ambience that came from living in such a place, or were so fond of the laidback lifestyle that came from living in such a setting that they had more sense than to move.

That's it. The mindset. It's the mindset that allows people to think differently about having all the conveniences of a bank or shopping strip on every corner, or being five minutes away from their job. These people are satisfied with who they are and where they are, and they're able to "stop and smell the roses" all the way from home each day to the grocery store or work.

Talitha gave a long, slow sigh thinking how very different this was from any lifestyle she'd ever known. *But what a blessed lifestyle this seems to be.* She looked at the people who sat around her. *Could I ever be content to live in a place like this permanently?*

The Cedar Mountain Hardware store was all she expected and more. Talitha noticed the Liar's Corner immediately to the right as soon as she walked through the front door. *That's it. Trap 'em the second they walk in the place.* It seemed funny to see men sitting in the corner of the hardware store while the wives were the ones doing the shopping. *Totally opposite from the huge home improvement stores back home.*

The setting was exactly as it had been photographed in the *Transylvania Times.* There was a checkerboard atop a barrel, and an oversized rocker big enough for anyone to sit in. Several animals native to the area had been stuffed and were placed throughout the Liar's Corner.

Talitha took a seat in one of the rockers and listened as the old-timers and the visitors sat around the checkerboards. *This is great. The place isn't open for business yet and already it's attracting visitors and claiming regulars!*

She looked up at a huge saw hanging from the back wall of the corner section. "That saw's cut many a tree in Cedar Mountain. Belonged to my grandpa," one of the checker players stated after noticing Talitha's stare.

"Watch out, or he'll be telling you that there's the one that cut down that tree that's claimed to have provided all the wood for that church down the road. Why, that tale's better than a Paul Bunyan story," kidded another checker player.

"So the bit about one tree being big enough for all that wood at the church is a legend?" Talitha asked, glad to hear it from someone besides Modena. *I can tell her she didn't let the cat out of the bag.*

"Hey, did you hear that?" piped up another of the checker

players. "We done gone and got ourselves a legend here in Cedar Mountain."

"Bud, I suspect these hills are full of many a legend," replied the first checker player. "That giant map up there beside the saw so's ever'one who stops here can see where they've come from or where they're a-goin'."

"Oh," Talitha commented. She was halfway listening to a couple of men standing underneath the map talking about where they both visited and trying to boast about who'd driven the farthest in the shortest distance of time. "Seems to be working," she observed.

What an ingenious diversion. While the women are shopping in all these little stores and figuring out where they want to go, the men can sit a spell and chew the fat. Talitha chuckled to herself. "Sit a spell and chew the fat?" *Where'd that come from? I've got more of my grandfather's traits than I thought I did. He'd be proud of me. I'm going to fit right in up here in these mountains, after all.*

"What are you doing in here, neighbor?"

Talitha turned in the direction of the familiar voice to see Flora with her arms full of light bulbs and several other household items.

"How about a game of checkers?" Flora piled all her intended purchases on the counter and headed for an empty checkerboard.

"I haven't played checkers since I was a little girl and then I only played with my grandfather."

"Well, there's no time like the present to start back. Besides, you can't come in here without playing a game."

Talitha decided a friendly game of checkers might be fun.

She was holding her own until Mack came over.

"I see you made it here," he welcomed.

"She didn't just make it here, she's making herself right at home," snickered one of the checker players who'd spoken to her earlier.

"So I see."

"It's your turn," admonished Flora. "Would you hurry up? I've gotta get home with Burrell's light bulbs."

Talitha looked down at the board to see several of her men had been jumped and one of Flora's was now crowned. "Hey' you cheated!"

All of the men in the corner howled with laughter.

"I thought that's how it got it's name of the 'Liar's Corner!'" defended Flora.

Talitha looked at the jovial expressions on the elderly men seated around her and the twinkle in Flora's eye at her impish game and realized that she'd just passed another phase of the induction process into the Cedar Mountain community.

"Great game, Talitha! I'd better get these things back to Burrell."

"Tell him you cheated at checkers when you get there," called the newcomer. "Or better yet, I'll tell him when I get home. Race you."

With that, Talitha tore out the front door, jumped in her car and took off toward Reasonover Road. She knew she'd be halfway home before Flora paid for her purchases. By the time Flora got home, Burrell would already have heard the story of the checker match. She could hardly wait to see the fake "reprimand" her neighbor would get.

That thought made her think of Denver and all his stories. She could picture him sitting in the back of Liar's Corner in the big rocker with everyone else, especially children, gathered 'round his feet and listening to all the yarns he could spin. *Cedar Mountain legends*, Talitha corrected herself.

A big smile spread across her face as she whipped into the shared driveway. *Perhaps I can talk Burrell into sitting on the front porch swing and giving me some more local history lessons of the place.*

Chapter 19

"Yep, that was probably the most terrifying time in my life," shared Burrell. "I was only seven years old and it was real scary to see the entire mountain on fire and it coming right toward your house. All the men folk got together and come over and dug a deep trench right there across the street."

"What happened? Did lightning set a forest fire?"

"No, it's a pretty sad tale. There were three men out there in the woods making moonshine and a revenuer came up behind them. They'uz three of them and only one of him, so they killed him to keep from being arrested. Then they set the woods on fire to burn up the evidence. I don't think they meant for the fire to get out of hand like it did, but they managed to escape."

Talitha had two questions left, but Burrell didn't touch on either one of them. She wanted to know if he knew who the men were, and if they were ever caught. The one thing she'd learned is that if they wanted you to know something, they'd tell you. It seemed this story was to go by the wayside with no ending.

"When I was a boy, we'd have to take the clothes to the creek to do the laundry. We put a big, long stick through the holes in the side of the wash pot so we could tip it over to pour the water out without getting burnt." Burrell took Talitha for a walk down through the thicket to show her where all the stories had happened.

"This is where Dot would sit and read. She'd be down here doing the laundry and get so caught up in her books that Mama would have to send me down here to get her. She'd have stayed down there all night if we'd of let her."

"The girls would go down there and lay out a house with sticks. That was where they played a lot of the time."

The next round of stories dealt with Burrell and Doug and their cars. "It'd be so foggy some nights coming up Caesar's Head that one of us would have to hang out the window or sit on the hood to call out directions, and the other would have to drive."

"How did you keep from having wrecks?"

"Oh, we all had our share of wrecks. There's been a lot of lives claimed out on 276."

Talitha was not surprised, for she'd already learned a healthy respect for the mountain roads.

"Back then, we had a big porch on the back of the house

and every night after dinner, we'd sit on the porch and watch the sunset and the moon come up. That was our entertainment every single evening. I loved the sunsets in the wintertime. Those were always the most beautiful. Now if you go up to Todd's home place, you can see what we used to be able to see."

After an hour or so of "back when" stories from Burrell, Talitha went home to type. She had already grown fond of sitting with her laptop on the front porch. Leaning back in her chair, she heard a humming sound and looked up. A bright green humming-bird was flitting right in front of her, less than three feet away, sucking from the red honeysuckle on the arbor.

Talitha froze. She couldn't believe how close she was to this creature. All her life, she had been intrigued by humming-birds and now, here she was almost within reach of one.

Too bad I don't have my camera. She dared not move, but knew that she'd be prepared from now on. Suddenly, her mind went off on a new tangent. *Think of all the nature articles I can do right here from my very own front porch. Flowers, birds, a white squirrel, bears . . .*

The story on which she had been working got lost in the shuffle as she again looked at the spectacular view surrounding her - much of it visible from where she sat. There was not one single place in her yard or on her porches where there was not a story, just waiting to be written.

Talitha jumped from the chair, took the laptop inside and returned with a legal pad and pen. *Ah! Feels like the old days when I was still a reporter.* She went about looking at things from a different point of view, selecting perfect shots for nature articles. *No wonder so many artists live secluded in these Blue Ridge Mountains.*

Her shopping list for the evening had grown to include several rolls of film. When the sun was right, she would be prepared to have photos to go with her stories.

Thunder and lightning quickly ended her imaginative spurt. She couldn't believe the difference in the reverberation of the natural elements in these mountains. *Nor how fast they creep up,* she noticed, quickly gathering her laptop, chair and notes before the rain pelted down on her.

Talitha wandered back into her house and looked at all the ways Burrell and Flora had prepared for her arrival. *Right down to the paper towels that say, "Home, Sweet Home."*

For the writer, she had termed this the year of discovery. There was something going on with her besides the money. And she was feeling more and more that the voice that had appeared recently had a lot to do with that discovery.

Chapter 20

"Why did I have to make that doctor's appointment so early?" Talitha was screaming at herself. *It's not safe to be out in this fog, I haven't eaten breakfast. Thank goodness there is one restaurant in Cedar Mountain.*

She pulled the phone directory from the drawer and looked up the number for Grammy's. *At least it will be perfect timing. I can be there at exactly the time it will take them to get my order ready.*

"C'mon, answer the phone," she said into thin air. "I don't have all day."

"Hello."

It's about time. "I'd like a ham biscuit to go, please. My name is Slagle and I'll be there in five minutes."

"We're not open yet," came the thick accent through the receiver.

"Is this Grammy's?"

"Yes, it is."

"What do you mean you're not open? It's after seven o'clock."

"We don't open until eight-thirty."

"You serve breakfast and you don't open until eight-thirty?"

"You can call back in about an hour and I'll be glad to take your order."

"I'll be halfway to Charlotte by then. I needed something to take my medicine."

"I'll tell you what, ma'am. The biscuits just came out of the oven. Tell me what you want again and you can come and get it. Bang on the door real loud and I'll come and let you in."

"That's okay. I don't want to be a bother."

"No, it's fine. You'll just have to have the correct change because I can't open the cash register that early."

"Are you sure?"

"Yes, ma'am. Just knock real loud."

Talitha hung up the phone and didn't know whether she was more stunned at the fact that eight-thirty was "that early" or that the man was willing to make such a concession for her. *That would have never happened at home.*

When she got to Grammy's, she had her exact change in hand, plus a tip for the man's extra service. It was a Jamaican male who came to the door. *No wonder there was such a thick accent.*

"Thanks, Mac," she called, remembering his name from when he answered her call. "I promise next time I'll come during regular business hours."

"No problem, mon!" he smiled, giving her a taste of the islands rather than the early morning fog of Cedar Mountain.

The experience with Mac set Talitha's mind into a reflective gear as she traveled down the mountains and foothills. *Cedar Mountain is a different lifestyle. If the restaurant opens that late, it means that most of its year round residents are either retired and have no need for an alarm clock, or are artists who don't keep regular hours.*

She knew that there was a much deeper underlying current than what she had first suspected. When she first came to Cedar Mountain, the thing that stood out in her mind was that the place – the surroundings and its people - their thoughts, their mannerisms – seemed to be from a time gone by. Talitha experienced the kind of relationships among them that fit the norm of the forties and early fifties rather than the twenty-first century.

The residents here, for the most part, weren't bound by electronics glued to their ears or fingertips. They were bound by "the tie that binds." People were more important than things.

Her assignment called to her, but so did one other thing. She turned the steering wheel to the left and headed toward the end of Reasonover Road. There was no way she could leave Cedar Mountain, not even for a little while, without first making a visit to the place that had first drawn her to Cedar Mountain – the one place that Randy had said was at the heart of Cedar Mountain – the place that represented every other place in the world, as far as Talitha was concerned – the church in the wildwood.

Now what she gleaned, after spending some time here, was that they were not behind the times. They were the only place she had ever been that had been able to keep up with the times. The sanctuaries stood in the same spots they had for generations. The hymnbooks were the same ones they had first bought decades ago. The church was still the heart of Cedar Mountain – not like all the communities where the church had once been the center of town and the people's hearts. Not like all the communities where most churches were no longer the center of town – the steeples had long been upstaged by tall buildings and large homes – much less the center of people's hearts.

This place, in all the upheavals of the twentieth century, still stood firm. It was built upon the rock – not the sand. *Not just the rock or the sand of the landscape,* mused Talitha. *But the rocks and sand of people's hearts, of their minds. Of their pocketbooks!*

The church was still the heart of Cedar Mountain because the members' hearts, their souls, their minds had not shifted like the sands of time that washed out under the current of society. Their entire beings had stood steadfast in the turmoil of the world changing around them.

Ah, to be home at last, she smiled, exonerated that her heart was back in the right "place."

Not a physical place, but a spiritual place. A rocky place,

not a sandy place.

No place is so dear to my childhood, she rejoiced, thinking about her grandfather and how proud he must be of her right at this moment. *As the little "white" church in the dale.*

Chapter 21

The warm April air soaked through Talitha's skin, leaving it with the same fresh glow that touched the surface of everything around her. *Ah! To be a part of nature!* She had taken advantage of the open invitation from Ellyn and Phill to use their pond and the front porch of the cabin anytime she wanted a change of scenery.

And what a change of scenery it is, she mused, seeing the first signs of spring.

Where she had seen the twinkling reflections of stars on the water during the week she stayed here, she now saw a fish jump in the water and make ripples. Talitha was anxious to see if there were more.

She took her laptop and sat on one of the pier's benches. There was a canoe resting along the bank of the pond, but she was afraid that would defeat the purpose. She'd be using her hands to row instead of typing her article.

How did I ever sit in that newspaper office all those years? she wondered.

It hadn't been so bad. She loved getting out into the public to do interviews and away from the desk job. *I'd have gone stark-raving mad!*

She thought of Calvin and wondered how he was doing in her absence. She knew she wasn't indispensable, but they had developed such a camaraderie over the years that she wanted to feel he was not immediately able to connect with this new neighbor, Vina Bruner, as well. *At least not yet.* Talitha hoped her ego was not showing its ugly face.

She stood on the porch for a moment, making sure her clothes were warm enough for the light wind. The sun was shining so brightly on the water that she was able to catch the glimmer of fish swimming just under the water's edge. Talitha quickly rushed to the small pier to get a better view.

One, two, three . . . Talitha counted all the way to twenty before she stopped. *Yes, I would definitely say there are fish in the pond.*

The sound of water, rushing over the rocks of the waterfall at the back of the pond, momentarily drew her attention away from the laptop. Water was also pouring out of the drain on the other side of her pond, adding to the gentle flowing sound. *No wonder people put all these little fountains in their dens or offices.* The serenity created by the water was truly sublime.

Talitha glanced down at the water's surface to see a leaf floating by, so slowly that it hardly seemed to move.

What a peaceful image that created in her mind – to be lying there, effortless, and allowing some other force of nature to be leading you down a path. No need to control on your own.

She continued to stare at the leaf. It seemed to stop. As she stared at it, she saw that it had not actually stopped, but was slowly turning, changing its direction. The force of nature that was propelling its movement had now changed its course, and it began to float toward another edge of the pond.

Talitha continued to watch as it moved away, then turned ever so lightly again before drifting on a little farther in another direction. It floated to a place where Talitha realized that her shadow was in the water. She truly became like that leaf. She was a part of creation, just as it was.

And I could be floating along on a smoother path, giving up my effort to control everything in life and let something, Someone, control the paths of my life. She watched the leaf a little longer, noticing that it bobbed up and down with the ripples that were caused in the water by the wind. A fish swam by, gave a little jump, and caused the leaf to slightly bump up and down.

Her attention turned from the leaf to all the objects around the pond. Not things of nature, but things created by human hands

– the huge house of mortar and stone, the grape vine lawn furniture on the banks, the torch lights that graced the natural area where the furniture sat. The sun was so bright that the reflections of the objects were as clear as the vision of the objects, themselves.

She put the laptop down on the bench and leaned over the water's edge to see if she could see her own reflection. Not at all surprised, she did see the image of her face. It too gently bobbed with the ripples in the water.

Another fish jumped near her, causing the ripples to get faster and push toward her. The reflection shook as it floated atop the water. There was a little distortion to the shape of her face, but once the ripples passed, the slow, steady ripples again took over and her reflection returned to its original appearance.

All of the years of her reporting kicked into gear as she read between the lines of the situation. *Sometimes we, too, are thrown into a situation over which we have no control. We can easily get lost in all the shuffle or disturbance caused by that situation in our effort to take control over it.*

She looked in the water where the leaf had been to see that it was gone. *Or we can trust in the One who made us and ride out the tide, finally coming again to the peaceful state we once knew.*

Talitha noticed that as the sun was making its descent – three-fourths of the way toward sunset from the time it had arisen – the reflections of the sides of the bank met each other. The tall pine trees on one side of the bank were connecting with the reflections of the house on the opposite bank. And in the middle, her face and shadow were blending into it. The reflections of rocks on one bank and the pipe pouring water into the pond were spreading from one of the other sides to meet in the middle with the landscape of the opposite bank.

Again, Talitha made an observation, using the investigative skills she had honed over the years. *When things come at us from all four sides, we have to remember that we are still a part of the world around us, a part of God's creation, and that if we give in to the force - the power of God - He will prevail in the end.*

Talitha wondered if anyone was within view that could see her, but she honestly didn't care. It was like her body took over and did what it was compelled to do by her inner thoughts. She moved the laptop, closed it, and laid it to a spot where she was sure it wouldn't fall into the water. Then she fell to her knees, using the bench on which she had been sitting as an altar, resting her elbows on the bench and clasping her hands.

Oh God, I feel Your presence around me, beside me and within me. All these things around me are Yours. They are depending on You solely for their protection and their care. You have fed all these creatures of nature and You have clothed them - the leaves, the flowers, the birds . . . all for their seasons to fit the course of the environment around them.

Oh, God, please let me be like that, too. Let me give in to You, to Your Power and Your Wisdom that You will cloth me with those assets so that I may be an extension of You in everything I do. And may my words touch lives and inspire others as You have inspired me.

The writer took several deep breaths, letting the fresh mountain air fill her lungs and begin to flow through her, becoming one with her body. Although she had been a part of her surroundings from birth, Talitha instinctively felt her place in God's creation. She gazed up at the sky, mostly blue with only a few scattered patches of white, and felt that her face was reflecting on the rest of the earth just as it had been in the water a few seconds before. Smiling, she looked back down at the water to see if the reflections were still there. What she saw nearly took her breath away, for there swimming just beneath the water, so that they were in plain view, were two fish. There was a spotted fish in front with a beautiful iridescent white one following it. They looked to be exactly the same size and the same shape. The first one appeared to be shining and basking in its own God-given beauty and glory, while the second one reflected the beauty of everything around it. By sharing in the beauty of everything around it, the iridescent fish demanded one's attention.

I wonder if that's how God sees us when we have become anew in Him, she wondered.

She watched the fish swim away until they were completely out of view. "Thank you, God," she said aloud, knowing that God had not only heard, but answered her prayer, allowing her to see His presence at work in His creations.

Talitha gathered her laptop and writing supplies and went back to the screened porch where she deposited them on the table looking out over the water. The breeze was picking up as the sun continued to make its descent and the temperature was dropping. - one of the factors that made the mountains such a desired area - the beauty of the four seasons.

She thought back to the week she had come to stay here, at the former home of Percy and his sisters, when the weather had been so cold that it seemed she lost two days of work. What she learned was that instead of losing two days, she had been in a spiritual training session for the next step in her life. A training session that empowered her to do greater work and reach more people. Through the two days of training, she learned to trust that the words for her articles would pour out once her fingers hit the computer's keyboard. There was, however, a prerequisite that caused a slight change of plans in her work. Like the path of the leaf in the water, her life and her articles were taken out of her control. The result was that her articles had taken a new direction, as had her life.

She grabbed her *Writer's Market* and a bottle of water from her tote bag, sat down in one of the wicker chairs on the porch and scanned the resource guide for magazines that accepted inspirational articles. There was a story in what she had just experienced with the fish, and in recognizing the Source of Light, and although she knew there was no way to adequately capture it in words, she was going to do her best to depict it on paper. It was too beautiful to keep to herself. Talitha was aware that some things were meant for one's personal benefit, but she felt she had been given this lesson from God to share.

How proud Grandfather would be. Not only am I taking that leap to do what I've always dreamed of, but I'm also helping others at the same time.

A huge smile spread across Talitha's face as she turned to her computer and let the episode of the past hour pour through her fingers. As she typed, she also sensed that her future would not be limited to one type of keyboard.

Chapter 22

It had been a day of discovery. A discovery, *or more of an acceptance*, of the source of "that voice." A discovery of how she fit in the world of nature. A discovery of what it was about Cedar Mountain. And a discovery about the *real* inheritance her grandfather had left her. After a warm bath and a quiet dinner, even the job of unpacking seemed exhilarating, for there was a particular item she wanted to find - her old Bible, the one she'd been given in her third grade Sunday School class.

After two hours of unsuccessful rummaging, she settled for her grandfather's Bible, and climbed under the covers, Bible in hand. Inside, she found pictures of herself with her grandfather from her childhood. Talitha read aloud as her fingers pointed to all the names in the recorded pages of her family's marriages and births and deaths.

Her eyes stopped. She found herself staring at the entry with her grandfather's name. The date of his birth had been entered with a fountain pen many years earlier, but peering back up at her was the blank space of his death.

It pained her heart to look at the page and know what she must do. This Bible was more than just a book. It was a record of her family, her biological family.

Talitha went to her desk and found a pen. After writing in the correct date, which brought a tear of grief, she laid the pen on her bedside table and opened the Bible to another page.

On it were some notes, recognizably in her grandfather's handwriting. She recalled that he'd taught a men's Sunday School class and the passages marked seemed to be a part of his lesson plans. Feeling a connection with her grandfather through the Bible, she began to read. It wasn't long before a startling realization came to her. *This book just isn't about my family. It's about my "family."*

The proverbial "light" came on before Talitha's eyes. She felt a sense of pride and inner satisfaction as she thought about why those family records were recorded in the inner pages of the Bible. *The Book of Life. God's covenant with us. Our family heritage and history.*

She reached for her dictionary, the book that had served as her Bible over the past two decades, to see what trusty Daniel Webster had to say about the word "family." As she flipped the pages, Talitha reflected on her heritage, her history. Not that of her family's, but that of Talitha Slagle.

It wasn't that she'd been a bad person. In fact, as the Golden Rule went, Talitha Slagle was a pretty decent individual. But her life wasn't ruled by faith, or any sort of spiritual relationship. The writer thought back to her high school and college days. Then to her days of being a single young adult. She had been afforded the same opportunities as every other person. The same choices of right and wrong.

Granted, Talitha was aware that she had made her share of bad choices. But for the most part, except for the divorce, there had been nothing controversial in her life. *But there's been nothing that stood out, either.* She glanced down at the Bible. *Until this inheritance.*

She began to wonder what her life circled around. It had been her office job for seventeen years. Now that she was out of that situation and on her own, there was no office.

Well, there's an office. But it's inside my home. Her thoughts stopped. *My home . . . Home.*

Still holding her dictionary, she looked up "home." *I'll bet it says nothing about it being an office.*

Talitha recalled the cross-stitched picture that her grandmother had done before she died. It had a house, very much like the one her grandparents lived in, and a saying stitched across the bottom. "Home is where the heart is."

Ironically, it struck her that her office had been her home. *Not an office in my home.*

She closed the dictionary without reading the definition. *I have put my entire self into my writing for how long now? It has consumed my life, my habits, my very being for how many years?*

Talitha sensed a pang of guilt running through her veins, spreading itself to her whole body. *All those years I had to spend with my grandfather, to learn from his wisdom, to take pride in all the family stories. And I didn't do it.*

She laid the dictionary down and reached again for her grandfather's Bible. Leafing through the pages slowly, noting passages that had been underlined or had notes written beside them, she felt a tremendous lump in her throat as she whispered, "This was his home." A tear trickled down her cheek. "This is where his heart was."

She turned again to the pages between the Old and New Testaments that held the details of her family tree. As she read her name, the pang of guilt began to be replaced with a sense of pride. Talitha read each name aloud, seeing each face that went with them in her mind. The sense of pride was replaced with a sense of longing.

Talitha thought about one of her grandfather's favorite comments, "God does have a way of taking care of us."

She realized that God truly was taking care of her, and that there was a reason for her being here – *home.*

"And Talitha, think back on all the memories of your grandfather – his favorite hymns, his sayings, his wisdom. You *did* spend time with him. Very valuable time."

For the first time, she welcomed the voice as it brought a tear to her eye and a warm spot to her heart and soul.

The proud granddaughter recognized that she had been merely going through the motions of daily living. There had been no goals, besides making a living as a free-lance writer. There had been no focus or drive for anything other than the deadline for getting out the next article.

She looked at the Bible to see where the pages looked the most worn and that's where she turned to read. *The Book of Acts.* There was an old photograph that served as a bookmark several chapters over, a photograph of several men standing in front of an old white church building. She found her grandfather, as a much younger man than she had ever known him, standing in the front row. In his left hand was his Bible. The same Bible that she was holding.

Grandfather apparently had no lack of focus. He knew what was the driving force in his life.

She began to read in the *Book of Acts,* the same book as had her grandfather, in search of her focus, her driving force in life.

Talitha momentarily stopped her rambling thoughts and her search. She considered herself to be a reasonably intelligent person. Her line of work had called for her to be creative and quick to come up with mind-provoking details. *Or did I print facts that merely spoon fed the readers?*

The thoughts that had been running through her head caused her to consider her own perception of the things she experienced or that had surrounded her in the years before. For it seemed now that the sights around her were the same ones that had always been there - *like power lines and electrical poles, for instance* - but she had never thought of them in the same terms before. She'd never thought about how the Power was always there, in the lines, and with the flip of one switch, an entire house would fill with light. *With light. My entire body can fill with Light.*

"Theology, my dear Tally, theology," she could almost hear in Calvin's voice, providing the answer for her like he always had in the years past. *Calvin, my dependable source of information.*

"Well, he did point you in the direction of Cedar Mountain, didn't he?"

She beamed, thinking of all the wonderful leads he had given her over their years together. Not only leads on stories, but the things that mattered in life. For the first time, she missed hearing him call her "Tally."

I'll call him in the morning and thank him for this "lead!"

Talitha went back to pondering her original question. *My mind didn't change. It didn't suddenly gain a wealth of knowledge.* She smiled when she finally accepted the only possible solution. Like the source of Power, that perception had been there all along. Flipping on that "physical" light switch was like turning on an entire generator.

She laughed at the saying, "Light's on, but nobody's home." If only those people could objectively see themselves walking around each day in the same routine, missing out on so much that their bodies already came equipped with. *Like owning a computer and not even using the best part of the programming.*

"Body's home, light's off!" Talitha said aloud. She thought of all the people she knew like that, just within her old office.

Within a couple of minutes, she had composed an entire list of people with whom she wished to share this message. People whom she loved dearly. People who possessed many innate talents and much intellect.

Her mind busied itself thinking of how she could initiate a conversation without sounding like a "know-it-all." She didn't want it to seem she was looking down at them, or condemning them. Rather she wanted them to see the change in her and realize it came from something greater than an inheritance.

But it is about an inheritance. It's all about an inheritance! And not from my grandfather.

She thought about the words rambling around in her head. *Perhaps it is from my grandfather. Only the inheritance he left me was not the money, but the spiritual example.*

There's my answer! "What would Grandfather have done?" she screamed. Talitha had answered her own question of how to approach others with another question. *Granddaddy would have walked humbly among men, just as Jesus did.* Her grandfather had known the phrase, WWJD, long before it was coined.

Chapter 23

The words flowed as easily on the computer screen as they had in Talitha's mind. She was not a bit surprised that her next article was completed in just over an hour and that she was ready to pitch it to the editors of several religious magazines. The creative writer then changed the article's slant, reworded a few sections, and prepared to send it to several more secular magazines that featured inspirational sections.

Before she realized it, it was nearly noon and she hadn't even thought about lunch. As she opened the refrigerator to take out the leftovers, she remembered the ad for Twin Dragons, a new

Chinese restaurant in Brevard, which she'd seen the evening before in the *Transylvania Times*.

Perfect, a Grand Opening! I can do something for Flora for all the work she did to get this place ready for me.

A quick phone call received a positive response to her invitation to lunch. "Give me another forty-five minutes to finish up here. It's a buffet, so they won't close before we get there."

Talitha sat down at the laptop, ready to go back to work. The words, which had been flying from her fingers, had suddenly stopped.

"Lord Jesus, gentle Savior," she began. Her fingers stalled, hovered over the keys, in anticipation of the next batch of words. There was nothing but complete silence as she sat there. She uttered the phrase again. "Lord Jesus, gentle Savior." Talitha wondered where those words, that exact phrase, had come from. It was not the beginning to any prayer she remembered from church, and it certainly wasn't in her *Children's Book of Prayers* that had the little blonde girl on the cover, her head bowed and hands together in front of her face.

"Lord Jesus, gentle Savior," she said once more. *What is the significance of those words?*

She paused to sense what was going on in her body, her own natural flow of life. It was a gentle feeling, a peace and a calm. Much like the rush of the running water, pouring from the spout into the water causing light ripples, but at the same time, offering more of a tranquility for her being than a disturbance or eruption.

Just like God's love, pouring forth from that sacred fountain, cleansing us from all wrongdoings, all misgivings, all shortcomings, all . . . ALL . . . Period. Offering peaceful tranquility to our souls in the outburst of joy that comes from that overflowing spout of grace and mercy.

A hymn she hadn't recalled in years began to sing itself in her mind. "Come, thou fount of every blessing, hither to Thy help I'm come."

Lord Jesus, gentle Savior. She knew the meaning of the words now. *Jesus, my Lord, my Savior, the Father who cradles me and holds me in his arms like a baby, gently caressing me like a baby in a mother's womb in the midst of the pain and strife of the world.*

Once again, she bowed her head, sure that the words would come to her this time.

Gracious Lord, thank You again for the many blessings of this day. Thank You for coming into my life, NO, for making me aware of Your presence already in my life. Use this food to nourish my mortal body and may it strengthen me to serve You in all my days. Talitha paused for a moment, feeling more like she was sitting at her Grandfather's table, listening to him offer a blessing, rather than hearing herself at her computer desk.

"It's time to eat now, Talitha. There will be more words when you come back from lunch. Remember, I'm the One in charge now."

Talitha didn't question either the words or the voice. "Amen," she shouted as she grabbed her purse and took off to get Flora.

Chapter 24

"That was a first for me," acknowledged Flora.

"What? Eating Chinese food?" asked Talitha.

"No, going the day the restaurant opened."

"Guess it comes from an old habit of having to do a review on opening day. Calvin and I saw every new restaurant in Union County open its doors during the past seventeen years. Couldn't let this one get past me. Besides, I love Chinese food, and that was a much better price than a buffet at home."

"Someone must have come to see you," Flora said, seeing a bright pink balloon tied to the baker's rack on Talitha's front porch.

"Yes, I wonder who," Talitha replied, playfully glaring her eyes at her neighbor. She had, in less than a week, become accustomed to one of her two next-door neighbors showering her with surprises, and since she was with one of them, that only left Burrell to be the culprit.

As she approached the porch, she noticed that there was a statue of a fairy sitting on a stump and reading a book.

"Wonder where that came from?" speculated Flora.

Talitha looked at her gracious neighbor and shook her head. "Flora, you and Burrell are going to have to stop this. I know you care about me and are obviously glad I chose to move to Cedar Mountain, but I don't need a present every time I come home."

"That statue isn't from us, honest."

"Sure, you're not the fairy Godmother who brought me this adorable fairy statue."

"No, I'm not."

"I thought I heard you two out here," called Burrell, coming around the corner of the house.

"Thanks for the statue, Burrell. She's adorable."

"Well, that she is, but I didn't put her there."

Talitha looked back and forth between her neighbors to see that their eyes were sincere in their denials.

"All I can say," interjected Burrell, "is that I saw a station wagon pull in your driveway while you were gone and then a delivery truck."

The three of them walked up the ramp to the porch and spotted a box beside the door.

"See, I told you they weren't from us," defended Flora.

Burrell took out his pocketknife and cut the tape on the

box and then handed it to Talitha who promptly ripped into the package. Inside was a smaller box, a yellow sticky note attached to its top. She recognized the handwriting on sight.

"Dear Calvin. I can't believe he sent me something, much less this quickly after I told him about the cottage."

"Calvin, huh?" Burrell taunted.

"Calvin. That's a nice name," encouraged Flora. "Has a strength about it."

"Now don't you go getting involved," scolded Burrell. "You'll have to watch her," he warned Talitha. She's bad about playing matchmaker."

"Calvin is the man whose desk was beside mine all those years at the newspaper office."

"So if you're not serious by now, I guess you're not going to be?" questioned Flora.

"I'm not going to be serious about anyone, Flora. Calvin is simply a dear, dear friend."

Talitha read the note aloud. "Because I care enough, I used the very best recycled box I could find."

"See there, he cares enough," teased Flora. Her comment received a glare from the other two.

Talitha tore the top off the smaller box only to find a decorative bag holding something that was carefully cushioned in tissue paper. On the bag was another note. "My dear Tally, Hope you can find the perfect spot for these in your new cottage. You were like the music of chimes in my life, Love, Calvin."

"I'd hate to see what you got from someone who *was* serious about you." It was obvious that Flora was beside herself.

Burrell pulled Flora's arm. "C'mon, it's time we left."

"We can't leave yet. I want to see what she got."

Talitha unwrapped the tissue paper to reveal a set of wind chimes made from various pieces of assorted silver services that had been shaped into intricately designed shapes. "He knows how much I loved chimes. You could hear one of the downtown churches from our office at noon and I was always commenting about it. I kept a tiny set of wind chimes on my desk and when things got too stressful, I'd run my fingers across the metal tubes. There's something about that sound that's most soothing."

"And you've already got that perfect spot to hang them." Burrell took the chimes from Talitha and hung them from a tea-cup hook under the ceiling of the front porch. The wind immediately brushed the silver pieces against each other making a pleasantly distinctive sound.

"Oh, I'll love sitting out here and writing to the sound of those. Now it will both look and sound inspirational while I'm working."

"Here's a paper that fell out of the box," said Burrell, as he tried to coax Flora to go home.

"Oh, goody, there's more!" she squealed with delight.

"You'd think this is for her," laughed Talitha.

"Look! It's a poem," exclaimed Flora, peering over Talitha's shoulder.

"Dear Tally, because the little church there seems to have endeared itself to you, I thought you might like this. Vina Bruner, the lady hired to replace you, wrote it. Hope you'll like it. Oh, and by the way, no one will ever replace you. Take care."

Church In The Wildwood

Surrounded by God's beauty, Peaceful quiet and still,
A church in the wildwood sits upon the hill.

A tiny steeple reaches up above the trees so high,
In a peaceful quiet setting, God's presence is glorified.

Welcome lowly sinners, Through the doors of red.
For you our blessed Savior's precious blood was shed.

That you might enter through, By His Holy Spirit led.
And kneeling at the altar, Let your heart be fed.

Kneeling at the altar, down on your knees.
Your sins now forgiven, By His grace you're free.

"I still think he likes you," hinted Flora. "Why don't you call him?"

"I will, and thank him." Talitha's eyes flashed straight at Flora. "And that's all!"

As Burrell and Flora walked away, she called out to them. "Supper's at my place this evening. Seven sharp."

"I'll bring dessert," insisted Burrell, "so don't fix too much."

Seven came early in the midst of unpacking. *Thankfully this*

place was furnished. I'd have been unpacking and arranging forever.

Burrell knocked on the door precisely on the hour.

"You're in for a treat," bragged Flora. "Burrell made his specialty for dessert. Homemade fresh strawberry ice cream."

"It's a good thing I only made a broccoli casserole. When he said not to fix much, I took him at his word."

"I'd have never thought that broccoli and strawberries tasted good together," Flora said halfway through dinner, "but they're a great combination."

Talitha had to agree.

"And the casserole was just enough. It left room for the ice cream," replied Burrell, filling up a second bowl for each of them.

"I don't know when I've had ice cream this good."

"The secret is that I still hand churn it."

"Oh, wow!"I haven't had hand-churned ice cream since I was a little girl and we used to go and visit my grandfather. My grandmother would mix it up with fresh milk and cream from their cows and I'd get to sit on top of a towel covering the freezer while Granddaddy turned the handle.

After supper, they sat around the table and talked for a long while about how pleasant the summers were, and how even with the hard work of moving, it was quite cool.

"What's that?" Flora asked, having eyed an oddly-shaped leather case for quite a while. "It looks like a guitar case, but I've never seen any instrument shaped like that before."

Talitha went and picked it up, opening it to reveal a triangular, sharply pointed instrument.

"It's a bowed psaltery."

"You mean like David played in the Bible?"

"Not exactly. This one's specially made of purple-heart wood from Mexico. I seriously doubt that David had any of that back in his day." Talitha sat back and played the bowed psaltery, enjoying the richness of the strings that she'd long forgotten.

She was still unpacking boxes when the local late news took over the television screen. Talitha recognized Brevard's mayor and the owner of the White Squirrel Shoppe talking about the First Annual White Squirrel Festival on the local channel.

Sounds like something I need to check into. Perhaps there's a great article in this somewhere.

"We'll release a white squirrel and his antics will tell us whether we'll have a long, lazy day summer or an early fall," stated the mayor.

A quick pause was just enough time to hear all the particulars for the next day's activities to be held on Main Street in Brevard. "I really hate squirrels. They're nothing more than oversized rats with bushy tails, only with better PR!" she verbalized aloud.

Talitha could hardly believe her ears when the Late News was followed by David Letterman whose Top Ten List for the night was ten reasons why a white squirrel was better than the renowned groundhog for forecasting the weather.

"Hate squirrels or not, I'm going. Who knows what kind of article or inspiration I might find there?"

Chapter 25

"The visit to the festival was not only a welcome break from the laptop, but a chance to pick up some really good bargains in honor of the event. Vendors of every sort lined the sidewalks and the streets, which had been closed for the event. Talitha got a first hand glimpse, and listen, at the acclaimed musicians for which Brevard was noted. With all that had been going on, she had yet to get an opportunity to check out all the spots that Calvin had mentioned to her when he first suggested she check out the area.

A stop at the White Squirrel Shoppe resulted in some lace curtains for her windows and a table runner to match. She also stocked up on plenty of candles for the mild summer evenings.

She darted into the Celestial Music Shop to pick up two CDs of the Hogtown Squealers, a local band. One of the copies was for Calvin, to which she planned to attach a note thanking him for sending her to a haven of culture. The other Talitha bought for her own pleasure, along with a CD of a local jazz musician who'd won all sorts of honors. She'd hope to buy a season pass to the Summer Theater, but was only able to pick up a schedule of the shows and concerts. *Perhaps I'll invite Calvin up to see one of those. He indicated that he'd enjoy that.*

Her favorite find of the day was an antique book easel with weights on strings to hold the pages down. Talitha found it while combing through all the little corner hideaways in Kris' Klassics. The store had everything from new decorator pieces, and works of local artists and craftspeople, to rare antique pieces on consignment. She could have spent a day uncovering all the unique things cleverly displayed throughout the showroom.

Seems like I've found plenty of places to visit in Brevard besides Kelly's. Maybe squirrels aren't such a bad thing after all. I never knew I could learn so much just because of one of those little critters!

On the way back to her car, Talitha heard a man on a stage that had been set up beside the courthouse. He was announcing a contest for an original anthem for the White Squirrel Festival. She couldn't resist the urge to take a seat in one of the chairs that had been set up in the middle of the street and eat a funnel cake and hear the local talent.

She'd attended plenty of street festivals in Charlotte and the surrounding areas, even written about a few, but never had she been able to sit down, *in a metal folding chair, no less,* in the middle of the street. *How I love this small town flavor.* She downed the last bite of the funnel cake. *In more ways than one!*

The afternoon's writing break that was meant to last for a couple of hours went way into the evening. Talitha came home and immediately retreated to the back deck. From there, it appeared the moon was almost within arms' reach as it hung, barely over the mountaintop.

In stark contrast, lightning bugs were flying so high that they were over the tops of the trees. The sound of tree frogs reverberated with echoes from the mountains on both sides of the cottage.

No wonder Grandfather loved his mountains so much. Things look and sound different here. She thought about all the samples of pies and cakes and sweets that she'd indulged in at the festival. *They taste different, too.*

Talitha mentally tasted the tall stack pies that her grandmother used to make with dried apples. No one else in their community had known how to make those. She remembered, as a child, winning a writing contest with the entry of how her grandmother made the concoction. *Grandmommy even made one for me to take to class for an example.* A laugh joined the sound of the night air. *No wonder I won the writing contest. It was Grandmommy's pie, not my story.*

She'd never thought about it before, nor had reason to, but it was that lone incident that set her stars on being a writer. All of her hopes and dreams after that point were to be an aspiring writer, like Lois Lane, and meet some charming man that would literally swoop her off her feet.

Ha! All I got was Calvin calling me Tally everyday. Talitha chuckled at the memory. Her years as a reporter had been good ones. Nothing spectacular, nor that would stand out in her mind in her elder years, but neither a drudgery. *Actually the sound of Calvin's welcoming voice, with that name I abhorred, became a pleasant expectation each morning.*

Chapter 26

The long-awaited annual Fourth of July Celebration was all that everyone had promised it would be. Talitha found herself in awe of the number of people who came off the "hills" to join in this one location.

Wouldn't they rather stay home with their own families and have a cookout?

But as she stood taking on the reporter's role of the observant people-watcher, she saw that everyone here was one giant family. It didn't even seem like an extended family, but rather a large reunion of parents and siblings. *The melting pot extraordinaire.*

While everyone else sat in clusters of loved ones or stood catching up with old friends, Talitha wandered aimlessly across the fields looking back from the lake to the house and the barn that had been on this site for nearly a century. Children roasted marshmallows on a bonfire, played in the paddleboat or went swimming, each one finding a fun way to spend time until the appointed hour for receiving boxes of sparklers.

What it would have been like a hundred years before. When there was no electricity. Families arrived to Hendersonville on the train and took hacks, which were taxis, or horse and buggies to their hideaway.

She decided to let her daydreaming mind stop wondering and let her steps start wandering back toward the throng of people.

"Hey, there's the Saint Brothers," Flora announced as she punched Talitha's elbows. "Wait 'til you hear them sing. They're as good as anything in Nashville."

"Ummm," was the only response Talitha offered. She'd heard lots of singers and bands in her lifetime. *And families and friends who always thought they were good, no matter how bad they were.*

"See? They're going up to that big platform. They'll start singing directly," Burrell said.

Talitha looked around at the crowd to see that many eyes were focusing on the three brothers. *Apparently everyone here not only knows these guys, but likes their music.*

It wasn't but a couple of minutes until the three men began to sing *The National Anthem* a capella in the most harmonious voices she had ever heard. She stared at the singers in absolute amazement. They were all Flora and Burrell had predicted, plus more. When the brothers finished, she had never heard the like of whooping and hollering, and the round of applause from the three hundred fans was thunderous against the mountain backdrop.

"Why aren't they on stage?" Talitha blurted.

"They are. Don't you see them up there?" came Burrell's response.

Talitha couldn't help but chuckle at herself. There was a huge stage and platform that had been built specifically for this event, and yes, they were standing on it alright, but she was talking about a "real" performance stage.

"They did a recording," added Flora. "I told you they were good."

Before Talitha had a chance to comment, one of the brothers, who now held a guitar, stepped up to the microphone. Coming up behind him were three young ladies, whom Talitha quickly recognized as the daughters who'd grown up in the cabin where she'd stayed when she first visited Cedar Mountain.

"We're going to do a few songs for you this evening," the guy announced, "but first we've asked the Masterson sisters to join us in *Amazing Grace*. We call ourselves 'Beauty and the Beasts.'"

Laughter was as thunderous as the applause had been only seconds before.

The guy was right. Those sisters truly are beautiful. But the only "beasts" in Cedar Mountain are the bears, and even they aren't too fiercely!

After a concert of several minutes and a short speech by the host of the event, people poured into the food line. Everyone seemed to know the routine of this annual event that, for this community, took the place of week-end vacations to beaches or other parts of the country.

Talitha headed straight for the band to find out about their backgrounds and why they weren't pursuing their musical career. *And to get a copy of their recording.*

"And why did you doubt their talent?" she seemed to hear in a roar from behind the mountains.

She immediately turned her head to see where the voice came from but saw no one.

Hmmm . . . that's strange.

"You had a cousin, Red Smiley, who used to play on the Grand Ole Opry. He was on stage and he came from the mountains. Do you think that only people in big cities can possess any talents or make their impression on the world?"

Talitha spun her head around again. "Where is that voice coming from?"

"What?" Burrell was standing behind her, ready to introduce her to the Saint Brothers.

"Oh, nothing," she said, still peeking around. *Surely that wasn't God talking to me. I've heard people say he talked to them.* She followed Burrell up on the platform. *After all, he did speak to Moses on a mountaintop.* Talitha glanced around precariously. *But I don't see any burning bushes around here.*

At nine o'clock, fireworks started to light up the sky from the back side of the lake. It was a show comparable to the one

Talitha had seen in Charlotte on many July evenings. Childrens' squeals matched the whistling and bangs of the colorful explosions, and adults, especially the war veterans, got tears in their eyes. Silent prayers were uttered from around the field for the men in the military.

To Talitha, the final fifteen minutes were truly "the Grand Finale" in more ways than one.

Right before the party broke up, Michael took the stage. With the aid of the microphone, his baritone voice boomed over the side of the mountains, "Don't forget the monthly meeting at the Cedar Mountain Community Center tomorrow night. Our own Irene May, the woman who can take anything and make it look good, will be demonstrating many of her talents. Come out and learn a new craft and don't forget there will be a prize for the most original patriotic costume."

Talitha left the party feeling like she'd taken a nosedive back in time. *Perhaps that's the magical charm of this place.*

Chapter 27

"I've got the perfect story." Talitha nearly screamed into the phone from the excitement she was fighting to hold inside.

"Let's hear it," invited the editor who'd suggested she call back if she got her hands on another story. He had been greatly impressed with the ability she had to place a certain slant on the assignment he'd granted her a couple of weeks before.

"It's called, 'Kick the pig!'" she reeled. "It's how,"

"Hold up right there," warned the editor, worry already evident in his voice. "We'll have every animal control person and human activist in the world on our case if we print some wild story like that."

"But,"

"Is that what those yahoos down there in those hills do for enjoyment?"

"They did it at church yesterday," Talitha managed to squeeze between the editor's phrases.

"At church? Kicking pigs? That's as bad as snake handling! I've never heard of such a thing, and I don't believe I want to start now. Please, Miss Slagle,"

"But, Mr. Tensford,"

"I told you that you had an open invitation to call me with any viable story ideas. Your creativity and craft of writing are excellent, but if you have no better eye for what's feasible than this, then,"

Talitha knew that it was now or never, so she jumped into the conversation. "You don't understand. 'Kick the pig' is an expression, not an activity. It means to put something in high gear and get on with it, wholeheartedly, 'giving it all you've got' as they say here."

There was complete silence on the other end of the line.

At least I've gotten his attention.

"They did it at church yesterday during their 'special music,' as they call it."

"They kick the pig to music?"

"No, Mr. Tensford. They don't kick the pig at all. There's no pig there. 'Kick the pig' simply means to 'get a move on.' You know, like you'd say, 'get the lead out.'"

"Ah," Talitha heard coming through the phone, literally envisioning the editor's puzzled face relaxing from its distorted shape as he began to understand where she was coming from.

Much unlike a few minutes earlier when he thought I was "coming from" Hickville, USA.

"Like what we mean when we say 'put it in high gear?'"

"Yes, quite simply." This time it was Talitha who had the vision. But her vision entailed all of the city slickers trying to keep up with the locals on these curvy mountain back roads. *In high gear.*

Not a chance, she grinned smugly and then continued, "You need to experience these people one time and you'll get the hang of their expressions and their lifestyles." This time it was her that paused. "And the rich history and heritage that is the backbone of everything they do." *Whether it's a rich heritage of running moonshine or singin' and shoutin'.*

"Kick the pig, huh?" The editor mulled over the words, seeing them on the printed page rather than hearing them in the air. "You may be onto something here, Miss Slagle. I'll give you three minutes to give me the slant you intend to put on this story. After that, you'll either be 'kicking the pig' or I'll be 'kicking the door' behind you."

Talitha took a quick breath and spit out her words, the same ones that she'd carefully rehearsed in her head before the call.

In two-and-a-half minutes, she knew she had this "pig" wrapped up in the bag. *Or "poke" as they say in Cedar Mountain.*

"Okay, young lady. You've talked me into it." Hearing the editor's voice coming through the phone, with his choice of words, made Talitha think of the editor of *The Daily Planet*, or another comic book setting, sitting at a desk on the other end, with a vest on over his rolled-up long-sleeved shirt and a cigar hanging out of his mouth. "I'll at least take a look at your pig story."

"Thank you, Mr. Tensford. I'm sure you won't be sorry."

"I certainly hope not, for if I am, you'll be even sorrier."

Talitha was sure that statement was true. She hung up the phone and immediately rushed to her desktop, which was finally set up and had fast access internet service.

"K-i-c-k-i-n-g" clicked the keys as her fingers ran across the keyboard. As she began the rough draft of her story, the ambitious writer heard the music in her head from the day before at church. The special music when she learned to "kick the pig."

She couldn't help but chuckle as she read the words appearing on the screen. They had the old gospel favorite *I'll Fly Away* going so fast that they could have literally taken flight, she mumbled to herself, trying to type as rapidly as she had played the piano for the choir to sing.

Talitha thought back to all those Sundays she had gone to church and sat between her grandparents. She had no recollection of anything like that in her memory banks of religion.

"Gimme that old-time religion," she sang aloud as her fingers continued to move. Grandfather would have liked kicking the pig . . . "it's good enough for me."

Chapter 28

Talitha pushed the secret security code she'd been given and watched the massively decorative wrought iron gate slowly open and glide backwards to allow her entrance into the exclusive home of the woman she was interviewing for one of her two Florida articles.

Now this is what I call a serious home. Glad I decided to press my blouse at the hotel this morning. Wouldn't want to look out of place for the madam of this place. A soft chuckle escaped her lips. *This is quite a stretch from the back roads of Transylvania County, North Carolina. Hope I haven't forgotten how to act,* she mused facetiously.

She tried to recall all her notes about this self-made woman hoping they would allow her to find some point of common ground once she began the interview. It seemed odd that as Talitha made her way to the front door to ring the doorbell she found herself muttering a prayer for help.

Since when have I asked for help? Much less from God?

Her thoughts turned quickly from trying to recall that act in all of her years as an investigative reporter back to the questions she had prepared. There was a slight jumping in her stomach, something she hadn't experienced since her very first professional interview seventeen years ago.

What's going on here? she wondered as her finger pushed the button. *It's only another interview. Relax, girl, this should be old hat to you by now. Don't get freaked just because it's your first interview as a freelancer. There's no difference. You've already set up the appointment. All you have to do is show up, be pleasant, ask all the right questions. Old hat.*

The door opened with a burst of energy. "Hello. You must be Talitha Slagle."

"Yes," The writer held out her hand. "And you must be Leigh Daris. Thank you for allowing me this interview."

"My pleasure."

Talitha's eyes quickly scanned the view from the door, trying to build an "at-home" environment for her character. The eloquently, yet simply, designed town home was most inviting. Its Tuscan furnishings were perfectly situated in each niche of the layout, many nestled between columns, of the first floor. The cream and salmon-colored walls were the perfect backdrop for each of the accessories.

That's odd. Among the intriguing sculptures positioned on shelves or recessed in the walls were framed works of photography, most of them appearing to have been taken from the same location. *Wherever it is must be a sentimental place to Ms. Daris. Definitely doesn't match the scenery around here. I'll have to add a question about them to my list for the interview.*

"Could I offer you some water or a soda? Or how about some fruit?"

"Maybe a drink." It might settle this nervousness that's trying to linger. "A diet soda if you have it."

Ms. Daris reached into the refrigerator that matched the cabinetry in the kitchen and took out two cans. She reached into a nearby cabinet and pulled out one glass and a straw and set them in front of Talitha. Then she proceeded to open the can and take a sip.

"I got used to drinking from cans and it's old habit. But please help yourself to the glass."

Talitha pushed the glass aside. "I'll drink from the can, too. Saves time and energy of washing the glass."

Ms. Daris nodded. "Would you like to move to another room?" she asked, pointing to the sunroom and the living room. "The seating might be more comfortable than these kitchen bar stools."

The interviewer looked in the direction of both areas. The sunroom looked out over a lake in the backyard, and across the lake, the opulence of Universal Studios. Its chairs were invitingly plush all the way down to the soft choice of upholstery fabric. The living room hosted a colossal, yet subtly romantic fireplace with various shaped cutouts in the stucco of the walls that held large pieces of pottery, all matching the same Tuscan design as the other furnishings. The sofa and chairs looked as if they were stuffed with down-feather and Talitha was sure that one minute in them would insure not moving for the rest of the day.

"No, I think I'd rather sit here," she responded, shifting herself on the tall stool to find the most comfortable position. From that vantage point, she could see all the decks and patios of the house, the sunroom, the study, the living room, the dining room, the expansive foyer and the classic staircase. She felt the ability to see all of the surroundings as she asked her questions would add to her insight of the character of the woman seated beside her.

Ah, the character of the woman beside me. Trying to assess Leigh's personality from the few minutes she'd been inside this home, Talitha tried to shape her questions to fit this character. It was a ploy, designed as a most useful tool, that Calvin that taught her to hone right after her employment at the newspaper office.

"*You can't merely ask the same questions to every person in every case,*" she could remember him instructing from across his desk. "*Get past the pad of paper and see inside them. Really see them. Find a trait about them that you can build on and ask the questions from that perspective. You'll get a better article and they'll feel more comfortable talking to you.*"

Given that Talitha had been an investigative reporter and not a features editor, the people she interviewed weren't as apt to relay or disclose information. Most often, her stories centered around the bad part of a person's life rather than all the good they had done for mankind.

Now as she sat sizing up "the workings" of this woman,

what made her tick, Talitha had already assessed the sense of a female who was quite complex, yet a simple person. "A real person," Calvin would have called her.

Auburn hair - *falling past her shoulders*; intense brown eyes – *ones that see things most people miss*; tall, slender – *obviously a woman who takes care of herself in spite of the demanding business schedule. Loves cats*, Talitha noted from the Persian, the Himalayan and the Mongolian that had each taken their positions to watch this stranger in their midst. Her mental notes that would be added to the pad once she left the premises were already off to a great start.

Sharply dressed, *but in casual clothing* – *a black cashmere sweater with a fur collar and camel-colored wool slacks*, designer labels whose styles definitely caught one's eyes – *like her home accessories, the feel and texture of the fabric is important. A very neat and tidy person from the looks of these surroundings.* Talitha squinted her eyes slightly, a habit she'd somehow acquired that noted when she was ready to seriously begin her work. *But then, how much mess can one person make when they're working or traveling all the time?*

"Ms. Daris," she began, after taking another sip of the soda and placing her pen on the legal pad, aimed for action.

"Please," interrupted the gracious hostess, "call me by my first name. Leigh is fine."

"Leigh," she nodded and started again, "how did you develop your business into the empire that it is now?"

Talitha sat and wrote several pages of notes for later reference as Leigh told her all about her business and how it began from an idea, "a seed," into the nationally recognized entity that it was today. She was mesmerized at this woman's intelligence and insight, yet amazed at how humble she seemed to be.

That curiosity led her to ask the final question of the interview. "Leigh, do you mind if I ask where all of these photos were taken? Many of them appear to be from the same place."

"Not at all. They were taken in the place where I was raised. I'm sure you've never heard of it, even though you're from North Carolina. Cedar Mountain."

The surprised guest was glad she didn't have a mouthful of soda, otherwise she could have covered the woman beside her, as it would have surely spewed during the spontaneous reaction. "Cedar Mountain?"

"You say that like you've heard of it."

"Not only heard of it, I live there." *Talk about common ground. This is better than I could have ever asked for.*

"You live in Cedar Mountain?"

"Yes. I'm renting a lovely little cottage from Burrell and Flora Pope."

"Uncle Burrell?"

"Burrell is your uncle?"

"Yes, I'm his favorite niece." Leigh howled with laughter. "One of his favorite nieces. We're all his favorite, you know."

"Yes, I do know. He talks about all his favorite nieces and nephews, and other relatives. I'm sure I'm his favorite neighbor."

Now both women were laughing.

"He and Flora were just down here. They brought Mother down to visit. We had an absolute blast. They left only yesterday."

"Yes, I know. We passed each other on the interstate and said 'hi' on our cell phones as we passed. But this is where they were?" Talitha shook her head in disbelief. "I had no idea that they were your family or that this is where they were. I knew they were off to see a niece and take Burrell's sister. I just can't believe this. It's like I've never left home."

"Here," invited Leigh, as she hopped off her barstool, "let me show you my collection of pictures from there. I took all of them myself on visits back home. It's still exactly like it was when I was a kid growing up there. Never changes." She smiled. "When you live in a place like this, where there's something new every time you walk out the door, the staid security of Cedar Mountain is most endearing and refreshing."

"So I'm finding out."

"Then I guess you've met my mother." Leigh went on to tell the identity of her mother, causing her listener to go into a near conniption fit.

"I met her my first time at the Rocky Hill Baptist Church in Cedar Mountain. She gave me my own private tour of the Allison Deaver home."

"Ah, yes. She loves that old house. She's such a history buff and that house is the oldest in the county."

"So you must be the daughter she went to England with last summer?"

"One and the same."

"I can't believe this. I simply can't believe this." Talitha sat shaking her head. "This is better than the original interview. I can do an entire segment on this part of the story. Would you mind if I pitched this to the magazine editor as a series of stories – each a segment of where you came from, where you are, and how both parts fit together so harmoniously?"

"Be my guest. I'm thrilled that you not only know where Cedar Mountain is, but that you know my family."

"All of your family, no less. Your sister and cousin sing in the choir, your cousin lives beside me, your . . ." Talitha stopped in mid-sentence. "Come to think of it, I'm probably the only person in Cedar Mountain that you're not related to."

"That's a good possibility!" Leigh laughed again, like someone who had just run across an old friend and they were sharing stories of a common past.

Talitha knew she was not an old friend, but that the entire community was, and her visit was bringing glimpses and greetings of home with her, just as well as if they had been tidily wrapped in a package addressed from Cedar Mountain.

"May I take you to lunch?" Leigh invited, after looking at the clock to see that their reminiscing had lasted way past two hours.

"I'd love that, but I actually have an interview for another article about the hurricane damage and reconstruction. I'm going to Melbourne Beach to hopefully find some interesting individuals to give me some insight into that disaster."

"You should have no trouble with that. It was terribly devastated in the areas of that coastal region."

"So I understand." Talitha, who was still on the second floor from where they had gone to see all the photos, started toward the stairs. "I need to get going. I'd like to see some of the affected homes and businesses before dark."

"Very well, but I'd be glad to take you out. How about I at least fix you a sandwich? You're going to have to eat somewhere?"

The interviewer looked at the welcoming face of Leigh. Hers was a sincere invitation and a most appreciated one. Talitha felt that to refuse would have been most disrespectful, especially following such a productive interview.

"Thanks, I'd love a sandwich." With the acceptance came the remembrance of how jittery she had been standing at the door. *All that worry for nothing.*

As she watched the successful businesswoman retrieving fixings from the refrigerator, Talitha thought of her grandfather. She had never seen him flaunt any kind of worldly possessions, but neither had she seen him ever want for anything. And now he had made it possible for her to want for nothing.

So why was I worried about this interview?

"This is self serve," informed the hostess after laying out the sandwich items on a tray. "I guess you've had a chance to go to Kelly's in Brevard since your move?"

"Randy's the one who prompted me to take the drive to Cedar Mountain. I was eating at Kelly's Restaurant one day and was so impressed with the atmosphere and everyone there that I kept going back every time I got a chance. He told me all about Cedar Mountain that first day, but it wasn't until months later that I actually made the trek up the mountain to see it for myself. Now the entire community's like family to me."

The two women chatted for a few more minutes while sharing their meal. Talitha made her farewell with the promise of a rain check for another meal, in a more formal setting, on a future visit.

"Maybe you can even have a sandwich at my place the next time you're in Cedar Mountain."

"I'd love that," Leigh waved from the front door.

As Talitha backed into the street, she noticed a scarecrow and several other festive fall decorations perched atop a bale of hay. Orange lights sparkled in the trees of the front yard. *How did I miss that on my way in? Guess I really was terrified.* She glanced down the street at the other yards to see that the Daris home was the only one that spoke of "home."

Or maybe I'm losing my touch, she scolded herself for missing such an obvious detail that would have been the first thing she'd have noticed at one time in her life.

She drove up close to the ornate gate to trigger its release. As it swung back allowing her exit, Talitha realized what had been so strange about this prearranged interview. She had called Ms. Daris on a tip from a women's magazine, yet she had been the one to be interviewed.

But why? she pondered while making her way toward I-95.

Chapter 29

The reporter in Talitha had decided, long before reaching the Florida state line, that the best way to begin an article on the hurricane damage was to make her own assessment of the coastal area's devastation before choosing residents to interview.

She was soon out of Orlando and headed south on I-95, looking for a road that connected with A-1A, figuring the only downed things she'd see from the interstate were trees and signs. Her story would focus on the good of the people. *The good of the people who had come here to do volunteer work to help a "brother or sister" of humankind.*

Talitha stopped at Titusville and began to take notes of all the things that still appeared affected by the back-to-back storms. As she drove farther south down the main beach road, and then turned to some of the side streets, her heart sank at the number of homes and families that had been wiped completely out. Thankfully, the traffic was minimal enough that she had time to actually write notes as she drove. *Guess the people who lived here had to go elsewhere to find shelter.* She noted all the downed or closed businesses. *Or to find jobs.*

By the time evening threatened to fall, the sympathetic reporter found a public access to the beach. She didn't even know which of the small beaches she was on; they had all run together from one wave of destruction to the next and many of the welcoming and direction signs were still down. All that mattered was that she was going to watch night come and the moon stake its position in the sky. Everything - the water, the lack of traffic, the starlit sky and the large moon - all made it difficult to imagine the horrific evenings that the now-gone residents had experienced only two months before.

She got out of her car, took off her shoes and made her way to the sandy walk along the water's edge. It seemed strange to be the only person in sight. Talitha began to wonder about all the former residents and whether they would even return to this place.

Maybe they're only gone for the winter. Maybe they'll come back in the spring when nature has a way of giving the entire earth a fresh coat of paint and a facelift, when life is ready to start anew.

Talitha deduced how backwards that scenario was. This was the land for winters, the place where everyone escaped to avoid the cold weather. Now it appeared that everyone had left just at the time that many snowbirds typically arrived.

Man may be in the technological age, but he still can't control nature.

By the time she returned to her car, not only was Talitha's heart saddened by the loss of the coast. Her stomach, which had been looking forward to a delicious seafood meal, had discovered that none of the restaurants along the waterway had reopened yet.

Surely there are some places to eat out toward the interstate. She backtracked to I-95 in search of a place to eat. *I'll get a room in this area and then I can spend the evening writing the article about Leigh and putting my notes together to begin my interviews here tomorrow.* It was comforting to know that when she returned to Cedar Mountain, she'd have two stories done. *And one to tell of my own,* she grinned, recalling her unexpected visit earlier in the day.

After the fourth motel informed her that there were no vacancies, Talitha quickly tore through the pages of the visitor's guide she'd picked up on her way into Florida, while calling the number of every inn listed for the area.

"I'm sorry, we have no vacancies," was all that she heard from the other end of each of the phone calls. And most of the voices were clearly not of American descent. *I feel like a stranger in a foreign land.*

"Okay, God, I have one last number to try, and if I get the same response, I'll drive farther south to the next town."

She gave a muffled chortle. *Girl, it's gotten so bad, you've resorted to talking to God.*

Twenty miles farther down I-95 was a spot beside the road with two motels, both of them backed up against a tall dugout bank that looked like it had been excavated simply for the addition of the motels. *Surely there's a room here. No one would want to stay in this place. There's no restaurants, businesses, nothing to do – not one thing in sight.*

"Huh!" Talitha blurted. "This is even too far off the beaten path for someone from Cedar Mountain!"

The first of the two motels flashed its NO VACANCY sign on just as she got to the driveway, and no one even acknowledged her at the second. She pulled around the sides of the building and asked a man who was unloading his car how he got someone to the window.

"I've been staying here every weekend for the past six months. My dad, who lives right down the road, is very ill so I come here and stay to be with him. I have my own key with a standing reservation for Friday and Saturday nights."

"Oh."

"You'll be hard pressed to find a room around here now. Seems every motel that wasn't completely demolished is filled with workers trying to get the area back to a livable state."

"So I've noticed." She gave a disappointed wave and drove south on the interstate. Talitha was sure there would be a rest area not too terribly far away.

Her "not too terribly far away" turned out to be over thirty miles. But there was a large rest stop with lots of parking and round-the-clock security. Talitha moved the seat back and curled up under her coat, scooting herself into the most comfortable position she could find. *Much in the manner of a lap dog,* she smirked.

Her mind rambled through all the happenings of the day and how even being stranded at this rest stop seemed to tie into everything that had been going on in her life of late, and also in the direction of her future. And then she thought of the motel situation and Jesus' birth.

Wonder if there was a camel "chase for the race" back in Bethlehem during that week? "No room in the inn," she mumbled softly before falling asleep.

Chapter 30

At least I'll be able to see the sunrise, she reasoned, waking up much earlier than she had hoped.

Talitha headed south, only to find that the next exit for her to turn and head north again was nearly eight miles away. She drove as hard and fast as she could legally to get back to Melbourne before the sunrise. As she hit the bridge going over the waterway, the sun burst into a yellow-gold fireball above the ocean's horizon.

The absence of traffic made it possible for her to pull over to the side of the bridge and get a few shots as well as enjoy the spectacular vision.

There aren't enough "oohs" and "aahs" in the world to adequately express my awe at this sight.

She got back in her car and headed toward the beach, still determined to see the sun come up over the ocean. *If I hurry, I can still get some good shots.* It seemed no time before she was parked and on the walkway along the shore at Melbourne Beach.

"I guess you're here to see the sun, too," welcomed a man seated on the top of one of the benches, his feet resting on the benches' seat.

"Yes." She got her camera ready.

"It'll come up in just a minute."

Talitha looked confused. "But I just saw the sun come up. Where is it?"

"You must have been coming across the waterway. There's a spot there that just at the right second, you can see the sunrise, then rush here and see it again. Don't tell me you were one of those lucky ones."

She nodded her head, not sure if she was more surprised at the natural phenomenon or her gift of being chosen to see it.

"You got here just in time." He pointed to the water's horizon with a tiny line of fiery yellow sitting on top of the ocean. Within seconds, the sun, growing to resemble a ball of fire, rose to send ripples of a bright glare across the waves.

"I come here every morning, rain or shine, and read my newspaper from this exact spot. No two days are ever the same. This is, without a doubt, the most gorgeous sunrise I've ever seen. And it's really strange, because this time of year, we don't get many vibrant morning openers. The clouds are generally out this time of year, keeping the sky overcast, and they hide the sun."

He eyed Talitha carefully. "You must be a special lady to have seen the same beautiful sunrise, not once, but twice."

"Thank you," she responded timidly. "It would appear that God is trying to get my attention lately."

She took a seat on one of the other benches that lined the walkway. Neither of them spoke again for a few minutes as they both allowed the beauty of the moment to touch them in their own ways. Shortly, a couple passed them on the walkway.

"Wasn't it especially beautiful this morning?" asked an elderly woman who appeared to be a generation older than the man accompanying her. Before waiting for an answer, she continued, "I'm so glad I was able to be out today to see it."

"It's nice to see you out this morning, Mrs. Witherspoon," the man seated on the bench acknowledged.

"Are you new in the neighborhood?" the woman asked Talitha.

"No, I'm only visiting," and then she quickly added, "but I wouldn't mind living here. It seems quite picturesque."

"It is, but don't tell anyone. We love the quiet serenity of the place and we don't want it to become like the beaches to the south of us. They're all entirely too crowded."

"Like the cities back home, I suppose."

"Where are you from?" It was the first time the man with her had spoken.

"Just outside Charlotte, North Carolina. It seemed a long ride to there when I was a child, but now, it has grown all the way out to my neighborhood in the next county."

"Sounds like my neighborhood just outside Atlanta. I come here every weekend to get a bit of solitude. It's enough to keep me sane during the rest of the week in the rat race, and a peaceful break to spend some quality time with my mother."

"He's such a good son. I can't believe that even at age fifty he still comes home to make sure I get my exercise."

Talitha couldn't help but giggle.

"My wife died a couple of years ago, so I think this is our way of keeping tabs on each other," the son explained.

The giggle stopped. Talitha wasn't exactly sure how to respond. She was glad when the man on the bench picked up the slack in the conversation.

"Going down to the Blueberry Muffin this morning, Mrs. Witherspoon?"

"I certainly am. They've finally gotten their roof fixed to the point that they're open for business again." She looked at the visitor. "Have you had breakfast yet?"

"No, I haven't."

"Why don't you join us?" And then the kindly woman turned to the man on the bench. "And you're welcome to come, too."

"Thanks, but I've already had my morning cereal and coffee. I eat there most weekday mornings on the way to work, so this is my time to be alone while everyone else goes out to eat."

"I take it this Blueberry Muffin is a good place to eat," Talitha observed.

"The best on the beach," said both the seated man and Mrs. Witherspoon.

"I'd love to join you, but I want to spend a little more time here before I leave. Thanks for the invitation. That was most kind of you."

"Well, if you get down there before we leave, the invitation still stands."

Talitha smiled and nodded.

"We'd better go, Mother. Even though most of the people are gone until their homes are repaired, there will be people coming in to pick up their pies."

"Enjoy your stay," the elderly woman spoke before walking away.

"The Blueberry Muffin makes the best pies you ever put in your mouth," explained the man on the bench after the couple had passed. "People can place orders and come to pick them up. They usually have lots of pick-ups on the weekends, even from as far as twenty miles away."

"Sounds like I'll definitely have to check that place out before I leave."

Again, both she and the man sat silent for a while as he returned to his newspaper and she focused on her photography.

"I guess I'd better be moving along. I've got some work to do."

"Well, be sure to go down to the Blueberry Muffin and see if the Witherspoon's are still there. Can you believe that she is the only person for nearly six blocks that encountered no damages from the hurricanes?"

"Now that's what I call a special lady."

"You're right about that one. She was a school teacher, and just from knowing her in the neighborhood, I'd say she's the kind that every child needs."

"Thanks for sharing the bench with me."

"Hey, no problem. And thank you for bringing us a magnificent sunrise. Come back anytime. You ought to try to come back when we're back at our best, you know, after all the damage is cleaned up and repaired." He gave her directions to the restaurant, and then called behind her, "Oh, I almost forgot. Their sign, like everyone else's blew down during the first storm, so it's propped up against the front of the building. But it's bright blue with a patched roof, so you can't miss it."

She nodded in understanding. Talitha hurried across the street, anxious to try to get to the eatery in time to catch Mrs. Witherspoon after the tidbit of information about her. *She'll be perfect for my interview.*

"Do you have any thoughts on why you were spared damage when everyone else around you was hit?" Talitha asked, her years of background showing.

"I guess God figured I was too old and cantankerous to have to move."

The reporter laughed, for the woman seated across from

her was anything but cantankerous and was an extremely beautiful woman for her age. "You'll never make me believe that."

"All I can say is that there are some things in this world we can't explain." She laid her fork down on her plate and leaned in toward Talitha with a look of total seriousness. "And furthermore, I don't think God intends for us to try to explain everything that happens in this world."

Mrs. Witherspoon's eyes spoke of many stories – stories that she had lived during her years and stories that had left her with both happy and sad memories.

Suddenly, a face that Talitha recalled from several years past came seeping through her own memory. It was a face that she had interviewed. *A face of a woman who had lost seven members of her family during a worship service on a Sunday morning. A worship service where a tornado ripped through the sanctuary of an Alabama congregation on a Palm Sunday morning, killing many of its members right at the moment when the precious children of the community were walking down the aisles waving their palm branches.*

Talitha had originally gone to the scene of the disaster to interview some of the survivors of the natural holocaust. But when she arrived at the location where the church had once stood, its walls crumbled and broken windows covering the ground, and people all around with clean-up crews that had poured in from all over the country, her heart lost its desire and her fingers lost their ability to pour out a page of words. For mingled with the good Samaritans who had come to help were the surviving members of the church also helping and ministering to the individuals who had come to reach out to them. The Red Cross came to feed both the victims and the workers and they sat and joined in fellowship in a way that resembled a family reunion.

It was then that Talitha saw a woman whose face and eyes were wishing desperately to scream and cry out in desolate despair at the loss of her husband and sons and grandchildren. But it was a face that showed she recognized the fact she had a purpose as a lone survivor. It was a face that asked no questions but took what answer it had in her existence.

Mrs. Witherspoon's face was marked with that same answer. She and the woman from Alabama were sisters. *Sisters of a same Father.*

Out of a natural response, Talitha reached her hands to her face, feeling her cheeks. She longed to have that same blessedness she'd once experienced. A tear fell down her cheek and into her plate.

"Are you alright?" the elderly woman asked.

Talitha nodded and tried to produce a smile. She wanted to share her memory with this dear kind soul, but her lips remained glued together as she pursed them to keep from crying. *How can I tell Mrs. Witherspoon about that day? How can I tell her that I came home with a story, the greatest story I've ever known?* Her smile grew into a radiant glow. *And how can I tell her that I came home from that place with the gnarled hymnbook that had been on the music rack of the keyboard of a musician who had lost her life on that Sunday morning at worship?*

She had put the muddied book in a box and sealed it and placed it in the back of a closet. In her haste to move, she had not even noticed it or opened it. In fact, she had purposefully hidden it to keep from being reminded of the words that accompanied the gift. Now the words, too, stood in the forefront of her mind as she looked at Mrs. Witherspoon.

"I have a very precious gift at home," she began slowly. "Another woman who escaped harm during a most devastating natural disaster gave it to me." Talitha swallowed, hoping she wouldn't choke up as she recalled the face and the cut hands that placed the hymnbook in her own hands. "She told me that God gives us all a special gift or talent that's meant to touch the lives of others. When she found out that I could play the piano, she told me that she could sense that God would one day use that gift in me."

Talitha stopped as another tear fell. She thought back to the day she stopped at Blue Ridge Baptist Church and found the door open, the Christmas tree up and the tiny ornament of the little girl seated at an old upright piano.

That day was no accident. The day I met the woman in Alabama was no accident. And meeting Mrs. Witherspoon this morning on the beach was no accident. She reached her hand out and placed it on top of the elderly woman's. "You're entirely right. There are some things that can't be explained . . . only accepted."

Talitha noticed that the eyes of the woman staring at her now began to dance, glad that her young guest understood what she was saying. It was obvious that the stately woman recognized stories in Talitha's eyes, much as she had in Mrs. Witherspoon's minutes earlier.

"It was no accident that I ran into you this morning," came Talitha's revelation.

"My dear, I believe you're right." She patted Talitha's hand with her other hand. "But we both know better than to try to explain it."

"We'd better be going, Mother," interjected the son who had sat silent and allowed the two women to share the morning. "It's time for your hair appointment."

"Yes," spoke Mrs. Witherspoon. "It's been an absolute delight, Talitha. Do come back again and visit with me longer."

"Thank you, I will," accepted the reporter, sure that her words were not merely an empty promise. She fully expected to see Mrs. Witherspoon again someday.

"Excuse me," came the words from a voice seated behind Talitha. She turned to acknowledge the woman who spoke them.

"I couldn't help but overhear your conversation with that.lady. When you mentioned the tornado in Alabama, my ears perked up. I didn't mean to eavesdrop, but I well remember that Sunday. Our church here sent a group of workers there."

"Really?" came Talitha's voice of surprise, but with an expression that stated that she should have expected no less.

"Yes, and I don't believe this connection is a coincidence, either."

Talitha moved to another chair at her table so that she didn't have to strain her neck for this conversation.

"I heard you say you're a writer. Why don't you go down the street to our church? Our Director of Christian Education is also a writer and she's there right now. I'm sure she'd love to meet you and compare notes. And there's an Arts and Craft Fair going on there today. You might see something you like."

Within a few minutes, Talitha had bid her other new friend good-bye and was headed out the front door of the Blueberry Muffin in anticipation of her voyage to find St. Mark's United Methodist Church of Indialantic Beach.

Chapter 31

Just as she drove past it, Talitha's eyes spotted a brick structure that she recognized as a contemporary sanctuary. It was when she glanced back that she noticed the downed sign for St. Mark's on the ground in the spacious front yard of the church.

Great! I missed it. How did that happen?

She looked up ahead to find the nearest side road where she could turn around. *That woman said right down the street on the left and that I couldn't miss it. I can't believe that I could completely miss a church.*

As she whipped the car at a forty-five degree turn, Talitha

spotted a sign beside the road announcing a yard sale down the street. *Can't go home without a souvenir*, she reasoned. Rather than turning the steering wheel the rest of the way to turn back to the opposite direction, she headed toward the end of the street in front of her, which turned out to be a cul-de-sac. Just as she suspected, there were several people milling around rummaging through the resale items. There was a large van backed up to the sidewalk, its driver cramming everything he could into the back of the vehicle.

Probably nothing left, she mused, glancing at the car console's clock. *The early birds got here over two hours ago while I was watching the two sunrises.* She parked the car at the closest opening along the sidewalk and made her way amidst the crowd.

A short brass vase with intricately etched flowers caught Talitha's eye the minute she stepped out of the car. She walked over, picked it up from the table and took a long discerning look at the vase before placing it back on the table.

"Morning!" called a woman, sitting in the shade of the garage.

Talitha took her to be the owner of the house and the "lady" of the yard sale. "Hi," she replied.

"You down for the race?" asked the woman. "I see your tag says you're from out of state."

"No and yes," Talitha smiled. "I'm not here for the race, but I am from out of state. I'm actually a reporter, and like hundreds of others, I'm looking to do an article on the rebuilding efforts from the hurricanes."

"Well, you came to the right place," interjected another prospective buyer. "We've had plenty of damage around here."

"And there's plenty of reconstruction efforts. Every motel in the area is full because all the ones on the waterfront were completely destroyed."

"So that's why I couldn't find a room. I thought it was because of all the race traffic."

Talitha thought of the five words she had heard in Bible stories, and that she was sure every child who had attended church in their lifetime had heard. *No room in the inn.* She chuckled as she wondered if there had been a camel "race for the chase" in Bethlehem at the time Mary and Joseph went to pay their taxes.

That thought caused another chuckle. *And only a couple of hundred miles away, five drivers are at Homestead, also in a "race for the chase" for the Championship Title.*

"Nope," answered the man with the van. "Men are basically camped out at every inn on the interstate. And even some of those got a pretty good bit of damage."

"The ones on the water lost entire back walls and big chunks of roofs. Take a ride up the road. There's evidence everywhere from you see the debris piled up."

Unknowingly, the shoppers gave Talitha a lot of useful "fodder" for her article, as well as an understanding of why finding a room in the area was an impossible task. She shared small talk of Cedar Mountain while they shared tales of their area. Before long, she realized that she'd better hurry if she was going to find the church in time to meet Milly.

Saying her cordial good-byes, the visitor started back across the street.

"Hey, you forgot this," called the "lady of the yard sale."

Talitha turned to see her holding the brass vase.

"You might need this for your new house."

"But I don't have a new house," Talitha remarked.

"You're going to," announced the woman. "There's a glimmer in your eye when you talk about those mountains and that community. I'm sure you'll be an official resident of Cedar Mountain before long."

"I haven't paid for this yet." Talitha reached for her wallet.

"No need. It's a housewarming present."

"I don't know what to say."

"Say 'thank you,'" ordered the man with the van. "I need to pay so I can get to my next yard sale."

There was a joking smile on his face, but Talitha was sure that his comment was factual.

She smiled and waved at the yard full of people that she'd met and took off for St. Mark's.

"Excuse me, but were you just at the Blueberry Muffin?"

"Yes." Talitha, a somewhat startled look on her face, slowly turned toward the voice. Her mind's thought of "But don't tell me God told you that?" must have been louder than she realized.

For the woman answered, "No, but my friend who just spoke to you called to tell me to be on the lookout for you."

"News travels fast around her," Talitha said with a chuckle.

"For some of us since the hurricane, news is all we have."

Like at the restaurant, her mood changed with the somberness of the statement. *Funny how people around here can instantly turn a humorous moment into a total state of sobriety.*

"I understand you're a writer."

Talitha was so busy making mental notes for her article from all the insights she'd been given by the locals that she barely heard the woman.

"Huh? Oh, yes . . . a writer."

"I didn't even tell you my name, we got a bit sidetracked. I'm Milly Calhoun, the Director of Christian Education here."

"It's a pleasure to meet you. And I'm Talitha Slagle. I understand that you're a writer, also."

"I like to think of myself as somewhat of a writer. I have a new children's book." She began to walk toward one of the tables with Talitha in tow. "Here's my latest one." Milly picked up a small green-covered book with a duck on the front and proudly held it up for her audience of one to see.

Talitha thumbed through the pages and immediately asked how much. She reached for her wallet. "I'll absolutely have to add this autographed copy to my collection."

Now I'll have a second souvenir.

"Oh, you flatter me. And in exchange for the autograph, I'd love to pick your brain on what it's like to be a professional writer."

"Deal," smiled Talitha.

"But only if it's done over dinner. I'd love to have you over to my house for a couple of days. I understand from my friend that you had a rough time trying to find a place last night."

"More like no success at all rather than a rough time. I actually 'roughed' it in my car at the rest area."

"Oh, my! We can't have you doing that! What kind of Christians would we be if we didn't take you in?"

"But you don't know me."

"I know enough. You'll be my houseguest for a couple of days."

"I truly appreciate the offer, but I had planned to get back sometime tomorrow."

"Fine, then you'll be my guest tonight, and over dinner we'll share notes on writing. How does that sound?"

"Like a winner? What time is dinner?"

Milly laughed at the quick-witted response. "We'll let my husband, Ken, be the decider on that. Wouldn't want him to feel left out of all the arrangements, you know."

There was no doubt in Talitha's mind that she was going

to like Ken Calhoun as much as she did Milly. She could imagine the smile on God's face at all of the "non-coincidences" happening around her. *But how do I react to all this? I'm not exactly sure I like someone else making all my decisions for me.* The young woman hastily reprimanded herself in case she seemed ungrateful for all the wonderful things transpiring in her life. *No offense, God!*

Hey! I'm not used to talking to God. What's happening here?

Talitha realized that she was unconsciously following Milly around the room, meeting other artisans and nodding without even hearing what was being said. Her mind was completely honed in on comparing notes and sorting them into a mental pro and con list of how her life had been with her making all the decisions – *at least, consciously!* – and all the events of the past few months – *when there was obviously a "force" involved.*

" . . . and she makes these gorgeous stained-glass window designs." The woman realized that she was standing face to face with a woman who had a welcoming smile on her face and her hand outstretched.

"Sorry," apologized Talitha, shaking the woman's hand. "I was so caught up in God's handiwork around here that I was speechless." *At least I didn't tell a lie.*

Milly and the woman shared a brief conversation while the visitor looked through the book at the original creations. Talitha was not a person who was into angels, but this artist had the most inspiring piece of an angel. It spoke to her in a way that she'd never been touched by pictures, jewelry, or art before. *Is it nothing more than the magic of the moment?*

She picked up the piece of glass art and held it up to allow the light to shine through it.

"Oh," she gasped. Realizing that Milly and the woman had turned and were staring Talitha continued, "this is breathtakingly exquisite." She didn't bother to explain that when she looked through the image, she saw a multitude of angels, much like looking into a mirror in a dressing room and seeing countless reflections of one's self.

Are there really angels all around me? I've heard of there being angels out there taking care of us unawares. She looked at the two faces, both with concerned glares, staring at her. *Or are all these people who've been a part of the happenings around me while in Florida "real" angels on earth?* Talitha stared into the faces. *I've heard of that, too.*

"What's the price on this?" she asked, breaking the awkward silence.

"Fifteen dollars."

Talitha couldn't believe her ears. She whipped her wallet back out and handed the woman a twenty. "It's worth this and more."

The woman gratefully took the money and carefully wrapped the glass angel for the buyer. "Have a great visit with Milly. I hope we'll see you in church tomorrow."

"I appreciate the invitation, but I'll need to be on the road back home. I'm working against a deadline."

"Ah, writers and deadlines. I've heard about those. So I guess that really is the life of a writer?"

"Sure is. It's that deadline that's controlled my life for the past seventeen years."

"Perhaps it's time that something else controlled your life."

Talitha looked at the two women to acknowledge whoever

delivered the statement, but saw that neither of them had spoken.

This is one weird place. If I didn't know better, I'd think there was a ghost in here.

"There's one more thing I'd like to show you while you're in the building," Milly suggested.

Talitha followed her past a water fountain, but stopped when she saw a painting of the nativity hanging from the brick wall that led into the sanctuary.

"That's what I wanted to show you. It was done by a man in our congregation. He was legally blind from birth."

Now there's a story, Talitha noted, taking a long look at the large painting. It captured the emotion of the night of Christ's birth in a way that she'd never seen before.

"And he was blind?"

"Yes. He used to teach some art classes, but he no longer does that."

"How could he paint it if he couldn't see?" The visual image of that was impossible for Talitha to fathom.

"You see with your eyes. He sees with his heart and soul." Milly watched as the visitor stared at the painting. "Notice the expressions on each characters' face."

"I did. That's what caught my attention from the beginning. There's emotion in this painting. I mean 'real' emotion. Something unlike I've ever seen in a piece of artwork before." Her eyes never moved from the painting. "Does he happen to sell his artwork anywhere? I'd love to have a piece of it."

"No. This piece was done specifically for this sanctuary when it was built. It was a gift to his church. From what I understand, all of his paintings have been a gift to some place that touched the lives of others."

"Well, one thing's for sure. His artwork and talent surely touch the lives of others . . . mine especially."

"I thought you'd appreciate his gift, both the painting and his talent."

"I'd love to meet this man."

"You can if you stick around for worship tomorrow. There's a Men's Breakfast before church, they're doing it for the entire congregation, and he'll be here. He never misses a Sunday. Someone picks him up every week."

"Hmmm," Talitha mouthed, "that's almost too good a deal to pass up. The breakfast and meeting him."

"You'll have to eat breakfast somewhere. Might as well be here." There was a twinkle in Milly's eye as she made the comment.

"I'll think about it," Talitha offered.

Milly reached on a table beside the painting and handed Talitha a paper. "Announcements," it read.

"You might like to see what's going on around here."

That's when Talitha remembered to mention the Alabama story and the fact that this church had been a part of the volunteer effort for that church.

"And you know what's really cool?" asked Milly. "Some of those folks from Alabama are down here now helping with our relief effort."

"So it's really true that 'what goes around comes around?'"

"It sure is. You ought to stay and help our town feed the homeless for Thanksgiving tomorrow afternoon. It's going to be a huge feast. I'm baking a big turkey and making plenty of dressing for it. That will be another volunteer mission you'd enjoy."

"Wait a minute. You mean to tell me that with all of the people here who are without homes that this community will still do a big project like that?"

Milly looked at Talitha with a strange expression. "Just because we were struck with destruction does not mean that there aren't still others all around us who need us as individuals and as a caring church and community."

"I never thought about it that way."

"The hurricanes might have robbed us of a lot, but they did not rob us of the two basic needs in life, and those are to be needed, and to need someone."

Talitha pulled a piece of paper and pen from her purse. She knew that she'd just been given the premise of her reconstruction article.

It was not until Talitha followed Milly out of the parking lot that she noticed that the street on which St. Mark's sat was Shepherd's Way.

Why am I not surprised? She turned left onto the highway. *Seems this entire trip is nothing but surprises!*

Milly and Talitha spent the entire afternoon comparing notes of the publishing industry. It was one thing to find someone to take in a straggler, but for that someone to also be a sister of the same mind and heart. The only thing they didn't share was a same soul.

Talitha listened intently to the stories Milly shared of her life's experiences. They were the basis for her writings. With one ear attuned to her hostess, the other was glued to hearing the basis for her own years of articles. *Writings that were based on the misfortunes of others, or bad decision of others. Anything but personal experiences.*

She began to question whether there was any part of her inner self in her writings, whether she had offered any opinionated slant to her "babies." Sadly, she had to answer that she had written the stories, and although they had been factual and interesting enough, winning her several Associated Press awards, she was completely aloof from their words.

But I had to be, she defended, arguing with no one but herself - at least to her knowledge. There was one other Being listening to her defenses. A Being that was also giving her counsel for those same defenses. *I was dealing with serious matters. Matters that involved criminals, even homicides. There was no way I had a familiarity with those issues. Milly's writings are a part of her beliefs, her values. They are not serious.*

Suddenly, the ear that was listening to her own defenses seemed to pick up the frequency of another channel, another voice. "Milly was writing for children of divorced children. She was writing stories that told of a love greater than any love on the face of the earth. She was offering a chance for children to speak out, to recognize their emotional, and sometimes physical, hurts and pains and deal with them. You don't call that serious?"

The voice was so loud and booming that Talitha peered at

Milly to see if she also heard it. But from the expression on the woman's face, it appeared that the guest was the only person privy to that proclamation.

Both ears turned to Milly just in time to hear Ken come in from setting up for the next morning's Men's Breakfast and announce that he was ready for dinner.

"Why don't you choose the restaurant?" Talitha insisted. "Since you've taken me in off the street, tonight's meal is my treat. That's the least I can do."

"Would you prefer steak or seafood?" he offered.

"Your wish is my command. I have no preference, and besides, I want this to be your choice."

"Why don't we see which of the places has the shortest waiting list?"

"Sounds like a winner to me," Ken agreed, heading out the street.

Talitha was secretly relieved that the seafood restaurant had the shortest line. She was not a lover of red meat, but she would have never shared that with this gracious couple.

The meal was delicious and the view was even better from their vantage point of a waterside table. Dinnertime conversation consisted of stories of the hurricanes and all the terror they brought with them. Talitha's heart nearly broke as Ken and Milly took turns telling horror after horror.

"Even the big Presbyterian church in the area was severely hit. Their sanctuary was leveled to the ground."

That comment caused Talitha to take a big inhalation right at the time she swallowed, making her nearly choke.

"Are you okay?" Ken asked.

"Fine," she assured, covering her mouth with her napkin for the last few coughs. "I guess I wasn't expecting you to say that a church was struck . . . much less that they lost their entire sanctuary. Somehow I guess I would have thought that a house of worship would have been protected." *Just like I would have thought that time in Alabama,* she swallowed.

"Dear, God is everywhere. The real place of worship is in one's heart," stated Milly.

Talitha pondered those words for a moment. She understood what the woman was saying to her, yet in her mind, a sanctuary was a building that belonged to God.

Obviously, Milly recognized the confusion on their guest's face. "Talitha, you are right in the fact that God's children go to a sanctuary to worship. But God's children are walking around all over the earth. We are all God's children. In today's society, people worship in all kinds of places - in old grocery stores of dilapidated shopping centers, in schools, even on the beach. There doesn't have to be a steeple to make a building a house of worship."

"I guess you're right," Talitha agreed after a few seconds of letting Milly's words sink in. "I never thought about it in that way."

"Do you think they had steeples back in Jesus' day?" Ken

challenged.

Talitha looked into the man's brightly smiling eyes. "No, I guess not," she mumbled, trying to remember her World History class notes from that time period.

Milly looked deeper into the problem that was stalking the young woman's thoughts. She reached across the table and took Talitha's hands. "You do realize that in Jesus' day, believers had to find secret places to hold their worship. People tour those places today. The early believers had various signs to show those around them that that they were Christian."

"But you must also remember," warned Ken, "that they weren't called Christian back then."

"People, whether they are good or bad, whether they believe in a Power greater than themselves or not, those things have no bearing in whether they will suffer heartache or crises. There is no perfect world, and there is not world void of starvation, war, natural disaster . . . other calamities. That will only happen in God's time, in His perfect world."

Talitha had the distinct impression that she was the one being interviewed again. *Two days in a row. This is getting to be a habit, God.*

God? Don't tell me that I'm talking to God. It's bad enough that I talk to myself, but to talk to God . . . that's . . . that's spooky.

"No more spooky than all of the other incidences of this weekend," came a voice inside Talitha. *Don't tell me that's God talking back to me!* She listened to her sub-conscious, sure for the first time that an inner "Force" was the source of the words she heard.

Either way, the reporter knew she had landed on a lot more than any two stories during the course of the past three days.

And she knew what the first item on the list of agenda would be upon her return to Cedar Mountain. *A quest for a sealed box with a muddied, gnarled hymnbook.*

She took a bite of fish. *Of another occasion when a sanctuary was struck in a worse manner.*

"You look to me to be someone who respects their elders," Ken estimated once they were back at his home.

"Well, yes, I guess I am," Talitha responded, unsure of the approaching direction of this line of discussion.

"Then I'm ordering you to go to the church breakfast in the morning with us."

Talitha smiled.

"Besides, I've already signed you up. I took the liberty of doing that today after Milly told me we had an overnight guest." This time it was him that smiled. "We'd be a pretty rude host and hostess if we let you get out of here without a bite of food in the morning."

"Okay, you win," conceded the guest.

"You can decide then whether you want to go to church with us or not. I'll not force you to do that."

Hmmm . . . you can lead a sinner to the front door of the church, she snickered aloud . . . *or even inside the Fellowship Hall, but you can't make the sinner go in and worship. Sort of like a horse and water.*

can't make the sinner go in and worship. Sort of like a horse and water.

"A sinner and the Living Water."

It's that voice again! Enough already.

"We'll leave at 7:30 in the morning. That will give us time to eat before the early service. Then, if you still want to get on the road, you'll have plenty of driving time left in the day."

Talitha simply nodded. She didn't bother to tell them that she suspected that voice she'd just heard would also send her a message about the next morning's worship, as well.

Chapter 32

"I see you're back," welcomed the glass designer.

"Yes," Talitha responded, "I kind of got roped into it," Her eyes darted toward Ken who stood greeting people as they came in the door for the breakfast.

"It would have been rude for the Calhoun's not to offer their overnight guest breakfast," smiled the designer.

"And it would have been more rude for their overnight guest not to accept."

Before long, Talitha was surrounded by a number of people who recognized her from the art show and the yard sale the day before. She was being treated like royalty. *Like a King for whom there was no room in the inn.*

The woman she'd met at the Blueberry Muffin came into the Fellowship Hall with a man holding onto her arm. "I heard you wanted to meet this gentleman."

Talitha saw immediately that this was the blind artist of the nativity scene. "Oh sir, I feel so honored to meet you. Your work is . . . is . . . I can't think of a single word to describe how it warmed my heard. I literally felt like I was a figure on the canvas with the rest of the characters there on that Holy Night."

She took the man's hand. "Do you have any pieces for sell?"

"Oh, no!" he exclaimed, feeling his way into a chair beside Talitha. "God gave me this gift so I give it back to His people. Not that you're not one of His children, but by that, I mean that I give it to houses where His people meet."

"I understand, but I'm dreadfully disappointed. I'd love to have one hanging in my house."

"You can join our church here. Then you'd have my greatest one hanging in your house."

Talitha laughed. "You people sure have a way of driving home the fact that you welcome anyone and everyone into your midst."

She shared a few more minutes of conversation with the artist and decided to get on the road. The service was nearly due to start and she wanted to slip out unseen. As she moved toward the hallway to the outside door, she heard sounds of a contemporary band tuning up and rehearsing.

That's certainly a different sound from what I heard at church when I was growing up. Talitha peeked inside the sanctuary. To her surprise, members had already gathered and were busy fellowshipping together.

"Glad you decided to join us," said the woman from the Blueberry Muffin who grabbed the guest's arm and escorted her into the sanctuary. The blind man was still on her other arm as she chose an aisle seat for them to occupy just as the music began.

"Good morning, everyone!" welcomed a guitarist. "We're so glad you decided to join us this day, the day the Lord hath made, at St. Mark's United Methodist Church."

Before Talitha knew what was going on, people were moving around hugging, shaking hands and greeting each other in the name of the Lord.

"Do we have any first time visitors?" the guitarist asked.

Slightly embarrassed, Talitha raised her hand. An usher hurriedly handed her a yellow card. "Fill out the card, turn it in at the table on the way out the door and we have a special gift for you. A small token which is our way of saying, "Welcome to Saint Mark's. Please come back anytime."

They give out presents nowadays for coming to church. Boy, this is different. All I ever got in church was a spanking if I didn't behave.

The minister stood and began his message. "This is Christ the King Sunday, the last day of Pentecost."

Pentecost? What's that? I've been an investigative reporter for seventeen years and I don't know what day it is? Seems I've missed more than the church, Talitha recollected, thinking of how she'd passed the church the day before.

"Today is a day that represents Victory in the church. Next week is the first Sunday of the Christian year, Advent. It will be a day to make room in your heart for the Christ child. A day to begin preparation for the birth of a King."

Make room in my heart for Christ? What is he talking about? Don't I already have Christ in me? I went to church as a child. Wasn't that good enough? What more do I need?

"We fill our lives with anything and everything that we see as important, allowing those things to stress us and take over any time that should be for self, families and God . . . and not in that order," continued the minister.

Talitha, whose own ears were attuned to every word he was saying, noticed that not one person was moving nor did she hear any of the coughs that came when anxious boredom struck. *Obviously I'm not the only one who needs to hear this.*

"Before you leave today, I'd like to invite you all to come down to the large city park this afternoon at four. We're going to feed approximately four hundred homeless people and we would love to have a good representation from our congregation. Also, tonight, don't forget our community Thanksgiving service to be held at the Baptist church. It was to be held at the Presbyterian church, but after their damages from the hurricanes, the service has been moved. A little secret here. We always give our Thanksgiving offering for a mission project. This year the money is going to the Presbyterian church, but they don't know it. Don't spoil the surprise, but come ready to give in support of their restructuring. Their insurance leaves a huge gap in the deficit for their repairs."

The service concluded and Talitha made a beeline for the back door, her card in hand as she passed the table.

"Oh, I see you're a visitor," spoke a man.

Talitha nodded in his direction and saw that a woman was

standing beside him at the appointed table for visitors.

"Here," offered the woman, handing Talitha a mug filled with an assortment of hard candies, prayer marbles and a note telling about all the programs for individuals and families at the church and in the community. "We'd like for you to remember your visit to Saint Mark's."

A matronly smile on the face of the woman caused Talitha to pause and accept the gift. "I don't think there's any chance of me forgetting it."

The minister by this point had caught up with the visitor. "We're delighted to have you today. Milly tells me there's a chance that you might be joining us to help with serving the homeless dinner this afternoon."

"Well, I,"

"Ah, there you are," interrupted Ken, who had finished in the kitchen and was going into the second service. "Yes, we're hoping that we can keep her that long."

"Well, I,"

"We'd love to have you," invited Milly, who had by this point finished her duties and made her way to catch Talitha.

"Well, I,"

"Great! I'll look forward to seeing you again this afternoon. It will be a blessing for all of us. I can't tell you what a good feeling it gives you to be a part of that experience."

"Well . . . I guess that settles it," Talitha finally gave in. "That's only a few hours away. I can still drive a good distance toward home after that."

Why did I agree to that? I know I need to be on the road. Those articles must be done and to the magazine editor by Wednesday morning

"Remember I'm in charge now?"

Talitha's head looked from one side to the other. *Not again.*

On the way to Milly's house, she thought of the pro and con list from the day before. Once there, she took an afternoon nap, something she never did, but she was determined to get home after the dinner. *That extra hour of sleep will allow me to drive all the way through,* she reasoned as her head hit the pillow.

When the last person had been fed, Talitha stood back and wiped her brow. Slicing and serving over four hundred desserts in a few minutes had been quite a task - fast and furious to say the least - but a richly rewarding one in that she pitched in with four others and had it knocked out like clockwork.

"Come and join us," invited the minister from Saint Mark's to the volunteer servers. "The homeless folks have had an opportunity to have seconds and some have even had thirds and there's some left over food. Let's go fix a plate and join our brothers and sisters."

After having smelled the roasting turkey even during her nap, Talitha was delighted to get more than a giant whiff. *A small bite will be great.* By the time she reached the end of the line, she had a plate heaping with turkey and dressing and all the trimmings and a piece of freshly baked pumpkin pie topped with whipped crème.

She found a place to sit on a bench underneath the huge shelter. As she looked around at all the people dining together, the reporter realized that this was the largest banquet she'd ever attended. And it's in the middle of a place where much of the population was affected by the recent storms. Within a few minutes, she was deeply engaged in conversation with all the people around her, all of them socially, ethnically and culturally different in many ways, but all seated at the same table. Her story was getting many more slants than she had ever anticipated. She didn't dare tell the people at her table that they had become a vital part of her assignment.

"Aren't the bells beautiful?" asked Milly as she and Talitha sat in the congregation, each reading a book while waiting for the Thanksgiving service to begin.

They had arrived very early for Ken to participate in the community choir for the event. The extra time gave the guest time to reflect on all of the unexpected twists and turns of the time she'd spent in Florida and how they were blessings. She now questioned whether the same kinds of blessings had always been present in her life and she'd failed to recognize them, or if suddenly God was attempting to get her attention.

I'd like to think I was astute enough as a reporter to have noticed had things like this been going on before. Yet, it's hard to believe that all of a sudden, things are so strikingly different around me. She focused on the bell ringers at the front of the church. *And I certainly didn't hear those voices – that Voice – before.*

The service went off without a hitch, the music of the bells and the choir enhancing the evening, and a large sum of money was raised for the Presbyterian Church. *Without their knowledge, I might add.*

Ken took Milly and Talitha out for dessert after the service and then they went back to the Calhoun home to reflect over the day's happenings.

"See, aren't you glad you stayed?" quizzed Ken. "You'd have missed all the fun."

"And all the story ideas," agreed Talitha. "But I really should have left today. I hate to be in your way another night."

"Ridiculous!" stormed Ken. "It's exciting for us to have you. Who else here can say that you stayed in their home? When these articles come out in a magazine, we can tell everyone we watched it all unfold in your head."

"Yeah, go in the spare room and write a bit. We can tell everyone we watched you write the articles."

Talitha laughed. "And I can tell everyone I stayed in the Florida beach home of an author." She had to admit that she was glad that she stayed. Something was definitely at work in her life that had not been when she'd left North Carolina.

What? No voice? she questioned when she went to bed that evening.

Chapter 33

"We'll be looking for you to come back and visit," shouted Ken as Talitha started the car.

"I will," she waved.

"Be sure to send us a copy of the articles when you've finished them," called Milly.

"You can count on it."

She drove back to the bench where her adventure on this beach had begun, following that duet of the same sunrise, that is. Talitha took a few photos of this morning's sun coming over the horizon. The water was as calm as she'd ever seen at the ocean.

These shots will be perfect for my article. I think I'll title it "The Calm after the Storm."

A short walk along the water's edge gave her a view of the Oceanside of the buildings that had been gravely splattered with ruin. *Strange,* she marveled as she continued to put one foot in front of the other, compelled by the mass destruction that showed only from this side. Destruction that had torn through the back walls and completely demolished everything on the inside of the buildings. *This is exactly how we, as humans, are. We put up a good front, not allowing others to see what has hit us, often unaware, from the backside and torn our entire lives apart.*

Talitha imagined her friends, looking at her after the two most vulnerable times of her life – going through a terribly painful divorce, and losing her beloved grandfather. The divorce had been completely unforeseen. She had imagined the fairytale life of being married and having three children. *Not seeing my husband, who refused to have children, out at a restaurant with someone else while I was on an out-of-town assignment. And following my investigative reporter instincts to get "the rest of the story," watching them leave hand in hand and taking a taxi to a resort hotel where I found that my husband had weekend reservations.*

The sickening feeling of that evening, when she felt her entire insides wrenched in pain, came over Talitha again as she stared into one of the storm-stricken motels that had nothing left standing but a front shell. *This was me when I returned home and found the note that said he wouldn't be coming home and that he'd been having an affair with another woman for nearly four years.* "A woman whom he loved," the letter closed.

She wondered if this was also her husband, who'd come

home one day to find that "woman he loved" with someone else. Her natural reaction, when he'd called in hopes of finding a shoulder to cry on, was to tell him that he got exactly what he deserved, but instead, she offered to meet him a local coffee shop to listen to his sobs. *Exactly like the sobs I'd had less than two years earlier.*

Talitha was so lost in thought that she didn't even remember getting in the car to begin the drive home. The sign welcoming her to Georgia greeted her before she realized how deeply engrossed she'd become with the beach scene and details of the interviews, and how in the process of coming here to discover the necessary facts for her articles, she'd discovered more about the facts of what was missing in her own life.

A glance at the fuel gage told her that she'd better discover a gas station. While she was stopped, she decided to have the breakfast she'd opted to forego earlier. The fast food restaurant was so full that Talitha pulled into the back parking lot of the motel beside it only to discover a huge tracker trailer surrounded by a throng of people.

Wonder what's wrong?

She parked the car and again followed the investigative instinct inside her to discover that the truck was a hauler and that inside it was the car that had won the Nextel Championship the day before. So *"you're" the reason I couldn't find a room*, she chuckled, recalling her joke about the camel race in Bethlehem. It may have been the reconstruction workers that had all the rooms reserved, but it was definitely the race fans that had the restaurant parking lot full.

"Can you believe we're this close to it?" a man asked as she walked up beside him.

"Hmmm," she shook her head.

"My friends are never going to believe this," another chimed.

"Wait until I tell my boss. He thought he was so cool because he had a better seat than me. I can't wait to go back and show him this picture of me standing beside this baby."

Somehow doesn't quite resemble a baby to me, Talitha reasoned, watching this assembly cooing over this car like a group of women would a newborn infant.

Camera clicks were going off at a steadily rapid pace as fans and onlookers alike were taking turns being photographed with the winning car. One man handed Talitha his new digital play toy and asked if she would take his picture.

"Can you believe this? Those haulers are sitting at the tracks, ready to be loaded and haul buggy the minute the race is over. Why, they're outta there before the fans even get to the parking lot. I stood at a streetlight one time next to a racetrack, trying to wait for those cars, and out they came, one by one, out of the gate past the track area and onto the main highway, off to another race or the garage. I thought that was heaven. And now, here I am, side by side with the winning car. Oh, man, it can't get any better than that."

"Could you see those cars if they were encased in these haulers?" she quandried.

"No, but just the thought of being that close to them was like the greatest thing in my life."

"Hmmm," she shook her head again, wondering if he had children, and if so, what his deflated attitude had been at the times of their births when they didn't come out like a pile of sheet metal. Talitha handed his camera back, and then gave him hers and asked him to snap her picture. *I don't know about getting any better, but this will sure be a great story. Just think, I'm not even a sports writer, but I'll have a picture that hundreds of pro writers and photographers would give their eyeteeth to have.*

The man took the picture of her, then asked, "Hey, you know what the coolest thing is? This isn't even this car's regular hauler. They have a couple of extra haulers, I understand, and this is one of this team's co-sponsors. I think they did this so that fans wouldn't be all over this truck driver every time he stopped on his way back to wherever this car's going."

Talitha wondered if the truck driver was actually supposed to have this hauler open now for fans to see his "valuable" cargo. She looked at him, sitting sideways in the truck with the door open while he carefully guarded his "baby." The reporter in her couldn't decipher whether it was the male in him that had to show off that what he had was better than what everybody else had, or if he was genuinely concerned with giving all these people a lasting memory.

"Look at 'er. You know what they'll do, don't you?" the man continued, pulling her back into the one-sided conversation.

Talitha stood staring at him, rather than the car, completely flabbergasted by the education she was getting simply by being in the right place at the right time. *And Whose fault was that?* she wondered facetiously.

He continued, not waiting for her to answer. "They'll put this machine in the back of their garage and bring her out again next year when it's time to race on a track like the one at Homestead."

"Oh." She glared at the face of the man questioningly, trying to figure how a man past middle age could take on the appearance of a young child simply by having his picture made.

"I'd better be going," he said. "It's a long drive to Bethlehem."

"Bethlehem?" she screeched. *I knew there was a correlation to that "No Room at the Inn" story here somewhere when there were no vacancies.*

"Yeah, Bethlehem, P-A," he bragged, as he said the letters of the state out one by one. "I had to be close to a racetrack. That was the number one qualification for buying a house."

"Hmmm." This time she scratched her head rather than shaking it. *Yes, I heard you,* she answered before that voice that had been tugging at her had time to comment. *The title for this story is "No Room at the Inn."*

The man turned and walked away, still mumbling to himself and anyone who would listen as he told how he'd just experienced a dream come true.

"Who'd have ever thought I would be spending the night at the same motel as the Championship Car?" she could hear him still saying while shaking his head from side to side. "This is the greatest day of my life."

I'm undoubtedly missing something here. It's only a car. A piece of sheet metal.

"His master," came the voice that seemed to be a vital part of this trip. "Who or what is your Master?"

Talitha wasn't even surprised by the voice. She merely took a deep breath and got in her car, ready to put the rest of the miles to home behind her. *Oh well, I may not have gotten home by the time I wanted to, but I have an extra story – one that wasn't even planned. I'm sure I can pitch it.*

"And whose idea do you think that was?"

The ex-reporter simply shook her head and gave a light-hearted smile.

"I know, I'm not in charge," she answered aloud, glad that others couldn't see her speaking to a voice that no one else could hear.

"Wrong! They can hear; they just don't listen. They're the same as you all those past twenty years. Hate to burst your bubble, here Talitha Slagle, but you don't possess any gift that the rest of the world doesn't have."

Chapter 34

The parking lot at Rocky Hill Baptist Church appeared quite empty on the Sunday after Christmas. *Guess everyone went "home" for the holidays.* Talitha had learned that "home" in Cedar Mountain meant approximately two hundred people, all of them kin to each other.

She walked into an empty sanctuary and put her coat and purse on the side pew next to the piano. That feeling of being somewhere out of her element again engulfed the young woman. Having lived her life in the "big city," and visiting several big cities during the course of the past few weeks' assignments, had taken away the short-lived comfort zone of being in this environment.

"It's about time you got back," welcomed Bobby, a man who'd rib her about being gone too long every time she returned from an assignment.

This time she was ready for him. She grabbed his hand and shook it furiously, greeting him with the same response she got every time he saw her. "My name is Talitha Slagle."

Bobby burst into laughter, causing Talitha to immediately feel right at home.

Mary Jane, Bobby's sister, walked in with a large square box and a gold lame ribbon tied around it. "I brought you a little something for the holidays to say we appreciate all you do. Besides, I figure you don't get a lot of time to cook."

"Don't tell me this is your famous caramel cake!" Talitha tore into the box and saw the cake she'd heard about ever since her first visit to Kelly's. "Your cakes are known all over this mountain. I feel most honored."

"Thank you. I hope you'll enjoy it."

"I will. I love caramel cake, and every one says yours is the best."

Michael walked in just in time to see Talitha placing the cake back in the box. "Did ya bring a knife?"

"No way. You get your own caramel cake," she teased.

"So that's the way it's going to be. Well see if I bring you any of Mama's famous fruitcake, or my Aunt Jane's coconut cake."

"Sounds to me like we need to have a big party," laughed Burrell, coming in the door. "And I'm going to be the first in line."

As Talitha sat at the piano, playing a prelude medley of

Christmas carols, she reflected on how different her life was from this time last year. *God, thank you for the gift,* she prayed, as her fingers glided over the keys in response to His blessing.

It was amazing how quickly the sanctuary filled, many people bringing family members from out-of-town. Talitha spotted Leigh Daris sitting with her mother in one of the pews on the opposite side of the church. Their eyes met and the woman whom she had interviewed only weeks earlier nodded and waved.

Talitha began to perceive the magnitude of this place, of the people around the globe it had touched through the lives of the people that had gone out from these doors, "witnessing and preaching the gospel." People who made the medical field more accessible for children at St. Jude's hospital, people who spoke to millions of race fans each year, and people who bloomed where they were planted. People who took the seeds that had been planted on this little mountain and spread them around every corner of the world.

A pride welled up inside Talitha with the realization that she was indeed a part of that crop, still in the growing stages, awaiting harvest and the ability to "feed others."

Chapter 35

"Thought you'd like to see this." Randy had come by to visit and was holding a five-by-seven white envelope. He reached in and retrieved a piece of paper. On it was a color copy of an old postcard. "Know what this is?" he asked, hoping to stump the newcomer.

"That's Ollie's old store," Talitha responded, her answer full of glee at her recognition.

"Yep," he nodded. "Years ago, the youth would go over there every Sunday night after church and beg him to open up and make us shakes or fix us ice cream cones. Not only was it a store, for he had a dairy bar down on this end," Randy added, pointing to the picture. "Man, oh, man. He made the best milkshakes in the whole world. That was back when Biltmore ice cream was the best out there. You can't get ice cream and milk shakes like that anymore."

Talitha imagined Randy, Michael, Regina and all their friends gathered outside the store after a Sunday evening service, yelling and screaming, picking on each other, but ready to attack anyone who'd dare touch one of the other members. A gang of cousins and siblings who were also best friends, who had grown up together and would be life-long buddies.

She'd heard tale after tale of all the things they'd done during their years of childhood and adolescence. Things that were quite different from the things she'd done as a child and a youth. However, there were those things that were the same for any young person growing up.

"Why don't you come over to Regina's tonight? We're all getting together and a bunch of the Gang will be there."

The Gang? Sounds as if there's always been a "gang" of some sort around here.

"I appreciate the invitation, but I'd better stay home. I've got a lot of work still to do on an article I'm writing. And I'd hate to be rude by eating and then taking off."

"Nonsense! Come on over and eat. There'll be enough food for half of Cedar Mountain."

Talitha thought for a minute. Perhaps hearing all the tales of the childhood Gang, with them all huddled around one table, would be fun. *Sure beats staying at home by myself all the time.*

"Okay, you talked me into it. What can I bring?"

"Yourself. Mama's making her to-die-for spaghetti sauce, Michael's grilling shrimp and scallops, and there will be all sorts of other things. We'll have more food than you can shake a stick at."

How I love all those expressions! She was already looking forward to the evening of stories and tales in another installment of "the life and times of Cedar Mountain."

He didn't tell me that all of Cedar Mountain and half of Brevard were going to be here. Cars lined the street and filled the yard of Regina's house. *I'm not sure I feel like making an entrance in front of this many people. I was expecting only family.* She saw that she didn't recognize most of the vehicles. *Why did I have to promise Randy that I'd stop by for a while?* Taking a deep breath, she now promised herself that she could eat a few bites and then politely excuse herself to go home and work.

Talitha hesitantly made her way to the front door and knocked. There was so much noise going on inside that they didn't hear her knock. A second knock produced no attention, either. *I'll try one more time and if they don't answer the door this time, I'm outta here.* She attempted to tap lightly on the door, but it seemed someone else had a hold of her hand as it pounded on the glass demanding immediate recognition.

"C'mon in," yelled Regina's husband as he opened the

door to an aroma of delicious spaghetti sauce.

The guest joined the large group of people who were all laughing, eating and obviously enjoying the merriment of each other's company. She loved the way they all told her to help herself and pointed to a long serving table, holding quite a spread. No one got up and hugged her or handed her a plate. They treated her like she was one of them and immediately she felt like the welcomed guest that she was.

"Be sure and have some of that spaghetti," yelled Michael. "You wouldn't believe how long it took me to grill that pasta. I've been slaving over it all afternoon."

Talitha knew the tales were going to be tall and hearty and that she would be going home with a richer understanding of the people and the community at the end of the evening. She took her filled plate, sat at the spot they'd shifted to create for her and listened intently as they rattled off yarns of yore.

"Hail, hail, the gang's all here," sang Michael as he stood at the head of the table and introduced her to everyone. He gave her their nicknames that had gone by the wayside with adulthood, but were still very much a part of their memories of each other. "Talitha, we all got together so you could see what growing up here was really like."

"I'm not sure I'm ready for all that yet," she teased.

"Anybody got any ear muffs? You might want to cover your ears for part of this," teased one of the guys.

"Okay, name check, Talitha," Randy challenged when they'd all been introduced. "Let's see if you got them all."

She quickly reverted to the memorization techniques she'd used as a reporter and began to rattle off their nicknames. "Let's see, there's Animal, Muncher, Spike, Clang Jane, Rat Fink." With that name, Talitha burst into laughter. "Every gang had a 'Rat Fink,'" she said through the chuckles. "That's what I called my cousin when we were growing up."

"See?" defended Regina. "Life here wasn't so different from anywhere else."

"Oh, yeah?" taunted Randy.

"And there is King Clod, Rauncher, Such-A-Boy, Pee-Wee, Plow Boy and Baby Face," she continued. Talitha looked around the table at everyone, some sitting, some standing, to make sure she hadn't omitted any of the faces. "Yes, I think that's everyone."

"Alright," shouted everyone as they burst into a round of applause.

"Looks like you get the door prize," congratulated Regina. "You get to wash the dishes."

Talitha beamed. She knew the laughter was not caused by what was being said as much as it was that this group of people had a love and appreciation for each other and were happy simply by being together. It was a contagious happiness, one that she could share in, even as a newcomer to the area.

"So now you've met the entire gang," announced Randy. "Except for one or two who've moved away. But they come back and visit a couple of times a year."

"They should have called us the Chain Gang," interjected Clang Jane.

"How did you all get from one place to another? It seems like you were always together."

"Most of the time we were," said Regina.

"We'd ride our bikes or walk or ride motorcycles," explained

Michael.

"Boy, I would have hated to see the bunch of you coming down the road toward me."

"So did everybody else," said Regina's husband.

With that, the tales began to rattle again, from one person to the other, each story triggering another one.

"Tell me about Denver. I love to hear Michael and Randy talk about Denver," requested Talitha.

"Denver!" screamed Michael.

"Good old Denver," commiserated Clang Jane.

It was clear from everyone's reactions that they all knew who Denver was, had spent much time in his presence and had enjoyed every minute of it. To see their faces and hear their comments, it appeared that this man named Denver was everyone's all-time hero of Cedar Mountain.

"I'd love to see a picture of Denver," Talitha stated.

"I'll bet Daddy's got one," offered Randy.

"We'll see if we can't dig that up," said Michael.

"I saw his grave out beside the church," Talitha said, her voice bringing a somber mood to the room that was filled with laughter only seconds earlier. "After hearing all the stories about him from Randy when I first visited Kelly's, I felt like the man was an old friend." She gave a slight chuckle. "There was a man doing some maintenance work at the church the day I was there. He knew Denver, too. I loved his comment about the day Denver found conviction. Said he never said another cuss word after that."

"And that's right," confirmed Michael. "I can remember when he got saved. Can't you, Randy?"

"Sure can. That was one changed man."

"He was always a good person," recalled Clang Jane. "We all loved him, the parents and the kids alike. But he was one more character. Us kids would go there every time we got half a chance because he'd tell us stories unlike we heard at home."

"And he'd give us coffee," added Randy. "We thought we's all growed up when he'd pour us a cup out of that old enamel pot on the top of his woodstove in the basement."

Everyone nodded and gave a smile.

"But ole Denver," explained Michael, "he was a hard one to catch. I remember Preacher visiting him and talking to him. Satan had a hold of that man and wasn't about to give up. And good ole Preacher, he saw all the goodness wrapped up in that man and never gave up on him, either.

"I'll never forget one afternoon when we were down at his house and Preacher came. Preacher asked him if he knew anything about the Bible. Denver grinned real big and said, 'I know that verse that says to do unto others and then run like hell!'

Randy shook his head. "Preacher didn't condemn him or anything. He simply asked, 'Now Denver, where'd you find that?' And that crazy rascal laughed and told him, 'In the second book of Henry.'

"That was the good thing," Regina pointed out. "Preacher knew not to put Denver down or criticize him for his ways. Then one day, it was like all those years of visiting and praying paid off."

"Don't you know all of heaven rejoiced that day?" Michael replied.

"They'd have workdays at the church and Denver was always the first one there to help," added Clang Jane. "Didn't matter that he didn't go to church. He thought that God's House ought to be the finest place on the mountain."

"My favorite Denver story is still the one he told Michael and me that day when we'uz still young'uns and had gone there during a big snow we had one year." Randy gave a chuckle himself. "We'uz all sitting in his kitchen, drinking coffee,"

"Our parents wouldn't allow us to have coffee," interjected Clang Jane.

"And this mouse came running across the molding on the wall and around to the kitchen cabinets and back down behind the refrigerator. Denver simply looked down at his watch and bellowed, "There goes Henrietta. Right on schedule.""

"Good old Denver," repeated Clang Jane. "God rest his soul."

Everyone held up their waters, sodas, teas, whatever, to share in a toast in tribute of Denver.

"Remember all those Sunday afternoons when we'd all meet down at Clang Jane's house? We'd pile on that hootenanny and,"

"Wait a minute," interrupted Talitha. "What's a hootenanny?"

Everyone else laughed, for they'd had the experience of taking a wild ride on the infamous hootenanny way back up in the woods off Solomon Jones Road.

"It was this contraption my dad made," explained Clang Jane. "We'd sit on this seat, and hold on to these cables. It would fly down the mountain and you'd hold on for dear life."

"Me and Randy and Clang Jane and a couple of other cousins would pile on, and it was like 'the Darlin's' from *The Andy Griffith Show* had come to town," roared Michael.

"And I'll bet you were just like Earnest T," joked Talitha.

Another roar of laughter burst through the room. Their new guest had made her own place into the crowd and was being accepted as one of them.

One of the younger generation of cousins, a girl, came running in the house complaining that one of the boys outside had hit her.

"Uh-huh," said Michael. "Same thing we used to do."

Some things never change. Then Talitha recalled the names Denver used on his wife. " You ol' widow woman," or "you ol' battle ax," he'd say. *And some things never stay the same.*

Chapter 36

The next day was Sunday. Talitha thought it would have been a perfect day to sleep in, but after the experience the evening before, there was no way she could lay in bed. A knock at the door told her it was Burrell offering to take her to church.

Isn't it strange that after all those times when I've refused to go, he still comes over here in this kind of weather? She thought of Preacher and Denver. *Thank goodness Burrell never gave up on me.*

She opened the door and informed him that she'd be ready by the time he got the truck warmed.

Huh! It's even stranger that he didn't seem at all surprised by the fact that I accepted the offer to go to church this morning.

Guess *everyone else had the same guilt trip,* she reasoned when she saw the full parking lot. Talitha was amazed to see a tractor parked on the hill behind the sanctuary, an indication that one of the men had gotten up early to clean off the parking lot.

"Someone's going to be really glad to see you this morning," exclaimed Alton, coming across the parking lot to greet her.

"Who . . . God?" Talitha asked.

Grabbing her by the arm and helping her across the parking lot, he turned back to Burrell and Flora. "Boy, am I glad you coerced her into coming this morning."

She wanted to inform him that her neighbors had nothing to do with it, but she didn't have time. Alton already had the door open and was proudly announcing that he had a surprise for everyone.

Ellyn turned to see Talitha and immediately ran over and hugged her like there was no tomorrow. "What are you doing here?" she asked, full of excitement.

"I can leave," Talitha joked, "if it's a problem."

"Oh, no! I've been practicing for over an hour this morning because our new pianist couldn't get here from town. This is a miracle. I just know God sent you here this morning." She took the guest's hand and pulled her toward the piano. "Now this is what we're going to do," not even asking if Talitha would agree to play.

I guess there's no use in me telling her I can't or don't want to do this, huh, God? As they passed the altar, the reluctant visitor saw the altar table with the brass cross in the middle of it. She gave a muffled sigh. *Just maybe God did send me here this morning.*

Talitha pulled off her coat, gloves and scarf and sat down at the piano while Ellyn instructed her on what to play.

"I've asked one of the Saint Brothers to play his guitar with me and I'll play the fiddle part. You come in on the second verse."

It was at that point that Talitha looked at the music to discover it was an old familiar hymn that her family used to sing at their reunions.

"A lot of bluegrass bands play and sing it, but I thought it would be really neat to use this morning after the great fellowship we all had at Bonnie's Hill last night," Ellen continued.

"Hey," yelled Michael across the sanctuary when he walked in and saw Talitha at the piano. "Aren't you too sore to be sitting on that bench? I figured you'd be standing for a week after that tumble."

Talitha laughed, as did everyone else around her, most of whom had witnessed her notorious tumble.

Michael came over and hugged her. "You're alright for a city girl, you know that?"

His comment caused more laughter.

Gee, this isn't like the church when I was growing up. If I'd laughed like this, I'd have gotten a spanking the minute I got home. This place is actually fun.

"Why don't you play something to get everyone quiet?" suggested Ellyn. "I'll go in the back and get the choir ready."

Talitha sat for a couple of minutes leafing through the hymnal looking for something she knew well enough to play with no practice. Her fingers stopped after a few pages when she saw a title she recognized. She closed the book and began to play the notes of *Church in the Wildwood*. Once the last of the choir members had filed in and Alton was in place on the dais, she concluded the prelude only to hear an appreciative round of applause.

Ellyn stood and told the congregation that they were to join the choir for the call to worship. When she began the introduction on the fiddle, you could feel the air of excitement begin to filter through the air.

"Will the circle be unbroken," sang the Saint Brothers, getting the service off to a rollicking start. Talitha didn't bother to look at the music. She heard her cue and hit the piano keys with a vigor that said, "I'm glad to be here today, God!" From the voices of the congregation, and all the stomping and clapping, they were glad to be there, too.

No one noticed the tear that fell to the piano keys as Talitha not only realized, but accepted, that she truly *was* a part of the circle of the "real" church in the wildwood.

Chapter 37

Talitha had spent the whole day dreading the New Year's Eve Candlelight service. *Why does it have to be at seven? What am I supposed to do for the rest of the evening until the ball drops?*

Even in her slack years of church attendance, she was aware of the "big city doings" for this occasion. All that knowledge came from being on the newspaper's staff. And where she came from, New Year's Eve services were more like watchnight services to bring in the New Year on the heels of the old one. Ending at midnight. So the way she saw it, the service was missing the boat from the get go.

Even so, when it came time for the appointed hour she was to meet the preacher, she took off out the door thinking back to all the wonderful things that had come her way during the past year, and all the things she was looking forward to in the coming year.

Nope, it's none of that "shedding a few extra pounds" for Talitha Slagle. It's going to be "land a few good articles and find myself a permanent dwelling." I'm going for the gold, the real serious stuff.

When she pulled up to the sanctuary, she wondered how many people would actually turn out for the service that was at the wrong hour.

"About that "wrong hour," Miss Slagle, keep in mind that things happen in God's timing, not yours!"

The voice again . . .

She walked in the side door of the sanctuary to find that the entire inner sanctum had been transformed into a U-shape with the communion table in the center and light trees and spotlights to either side against the wall. Candles were in each window and candelabras were at each end of the table set with the elements.

"Wow!" she blurted aloud. *This is pretty dramatic.*

"Did you say something?" asked the minister.

"I just wondered if I could help you with anything," came her answer as she stared at the surroundings in awe. "This is really something. I wasn't expecting this."

"Do you like it?"

"Yes, I really do."

Alton handed her the list music for the service. One of the songs was a little chorus she hadn't heard since early childhood

Sunday School days. Her fingers began to pick out the melody as the minister sang it. She played it again, this time adding an accompaniment and singing along with him.

Having made sure she knew the chorus, Alton continued, "For the song while they're lighting their candles, we'll use *The Light of the World is Jesus.* You know that, don't you?"

Surprisingly, Talitha did know that. It was a hymn she'd heard when she attended church with her grandparents. "I've heard it, but I can't remember how it goes."

The minister sang the first few words of the chorus and immediately Talitha fell in line with the notes on the piano. After the first couple of phrases, they were both at a loss for the rest of the tune.

Talitha reached for the hymnbook.

"It isn't in there," Alton informed her.

"I know it has to be in a hymnbook. I've heard it before." *How else would I know it?*

"It isn't in the old hymnal, either. I've already looked."

Talitha sat there for a minute. "Which old one did you look in?" She followed the minister to the choir room to see a book that was unfamiliar to her. "It's in the old bluish-colored Baptist hymnbook. Right across the page from The Lily of the Valley."

Whoa! she marveled at herself. *Where did that come from and how did I possibly remember that?*

The minister reached into a large pasteboard box and pulled out another hymnal.

"That's it!" exclaimed Talitha.

Alton quickly turned to the index, looked up the number

and found the page.

"See, there it is . . . right across the page from,"

"That's amazing," interrupted the minister.

Talitha looked at him as he handed her the book. "Yes . . . it is," she replied with a blank stare on her face.

The evening she had so dreaded, and feared would be a service of boredom, was already turning out to be full of surprises and "God things," as one of her former co-workers had called them when she had to interview people for the Religion Section of the newspaper.

Following the brief service of music and communion, the congregation, which was full, joined hands and formed a circle, ending the night by singing *Blest Be the Tie That Binds*. They then broke into an energetic group giving hugs to visiting long-time friends who had moved away, sharing resolutions for the coming year, but mainly, being one, big happy family . . . *God's family*.

Leigh stepped over to join Talitha. "Why don't you come over to our house for a few minutes? I've thought of a few more stories about Cedar Mountain that I'd like to tell you."

Talitha looked at the row of children and grandchildren that had come to spend the holiday with their grandmother, Dot. "Thank you, but I couldn't possibly. I don't want to intrude on your family time together."

"Don't be ridiculous. We'd love to have you."

Dot walked up and gave Talitha a hug with all her might. "The music was beautiful, as always."

"I hit more klunkers than I think I've ever hit."

"No one would have noticed," exclaimed one of Dot's guests, a woman whom Talitha presumed to be the one daughter-in-law since she didn't resemble the rest of the family. "To all of us, it sounded heavenly."

Talitha laughed inside. *Thanks, God*, she uttered silently, for she realized that it truly had been "heavenly." Every thing about this place for her had been "heavenly" – the way she found the place, the way she visited in the cabin, the way she found a home, the way she found the church, the way the church found her . . . *and the way I found all these new friends, who seem to genuinely care more about me than all of my old friends back home.*

"You are coming over to the house for a while, aren't you?" asked Dot.

Dot's son, Ralph, Jr.., whom Talitha had never met but knew, simply by his renowned voice and his energetic personality - as described by Michael, Randy and Doug - proceeded to give Talitha directions to his mom's house, taking it for granted that she was going to be a part of their family evening.

Talitha gave them all a wide grin. "Thanks. I'd love to come over if you don't mind."

"Dear, we'd love to have you," extended Dot with another warm hug.

Talitha walked through a small foyer, large enough for several coats to hang on the hooks of its walls, into a huge living area that opened to the kitchen beside it, the two rooms separated by a bar and stools. From the minute she entered its door, she felt like a kid in a toy store for the first time. It's vast coziness spoke of love and many memories. *With six children, it would have to be either love or hate, and no matter which one, loads of memories.*

The very thought of Leigh clogging around the room and shouting, "Yee-haw," was a mental picture that Talitha found most difficult to comprehend. Yet as she looked at the female business executive in this surrounding, she understood how the woman could so gracefully fit into any situation. *And why all those photos of Cedar Mountain hanging on her walls were so treasured.*

It was fun for Talitha, who had spent her life as an only child, to listen to the family rattle off stories of their childhoods and youth. She wondered if they were doing it for her benefit since Dot would drag out pictures to go with each telling. But as she sat there watching them bounce the stories off each other, she saw that this was how families held on to their heritage, to their cherished memories. Suddenly, she felt a strong sense of privileged gratitude that the Daris family had opened their arms to her and allowed her to be a temporary part of their circle. And as she shared in homemade fruitcake and other treats of the season, she realized that this was not a temporary inclusion, but a permanent one. She had just become the member of a huge family with a brother and lots of sisters.

As the Daris' continued to share fond memories, Talitha tried to imagine what it had been like for her grandfather, who had been the third of thirteen children, when he gathered with his family. *Over twice the fun*, she suspected, counting the difference in the number of children in the family.

"Won't you stay a bit longer?" they all invited when she stood to get her coat. "Thank you, but I'd better get home. I'd really like to be in my own place at midnight. I'm sure friends and family might call to wish me a Happy New Year."

She glanced at the clock in the car. It was ten minutes until the appointed event and if she hurried, she should be home in five minutes. What she failed to tell the Daris' is that she didn't want them to see her cry when the clock struck twelve and she was all alone in life.

But what about that family you just connected to? And what about all those people down at the church? You're not alone. Talitha was trying to pull herself out of her self-made pity party, but with little avail, as she envisioned the holiday evenings she'd spent in the past with someone she loved.

She shook her head in amazement as she turned into her driveway off Reasonover Road. An imaginary deep gravely voice, which she sensed could have sounded like Denver, scorned, "You spent too much time 'reasoning over' what you thought was to be!"

That's right, Talitha realized. *The only thing wrong about this evening was my comprehension of what it was "supposed" to be.*

A sudden movement caught her eye and interrupted her thoughts. *What's that?* A large critter of some sort was climbing the tree right beside her front porch. *Is it a bobcat? It's way too big for a squirrel.*

Her eyes reeled in on the object as she tried to make out what it was. As it moved from the trunk of the tree to one of the branches, Talitha saw that her company to see in the New Year was an opossum. *Wrong, a possum*, she snickered. *Not quite what I had in mind.*

She couldn't help but look up at the sky. *God, You're really making a point of getting my attention this evening, aren't You? Or at least letting me know that You're in control and that You do have a sense of humor!*

As she walked in the front door of her cottage, the phone rang.

"Hello."

"Happy New Year!" Calvin's voice sounded the same as it had every midnight for the past eighteen years.

"Happy New Year to you, too, Calvin!"

"So, kid, how have things been treating you? Are you doing okay?"

"Oh, Calvin, you wouldn't believe it if I told you."

"Why don't you try me?" came the coaxing voice from the other end of the phone.

"Oh, alright. It might be fun to tell you."

The beep of another call came through the line.

"Sorry, Calvin, can you excuse me for a second. There's another call coming through."

"Sure, no problem."

Talitha quickly punched the flash button and answered the second caller.

"Happy New Year!" came the unison voices of Burrell and Flora.

"Thank you, and the same to you," blurted Talitha. "This evening has made me even more aware that I'm exactly where God wants me. His time and His place."

She quickly got back to Calvin. "Okay, this is what it's really like here." Another beep. "Huh-oh, seems there's another call. Maybe my landlord forgot something."

"Happy New Year!" came the boisterous male voice when she clicked the flash button.

"Randy! How nice of you to call. Happy New Year to you and all your kin, too."

All his kin? That's all of Cedar Mountain, she wanted to laugh.

"Hey, Randy, thanks for making me feel like a part of your family and introducing me to the rest of the clan."

The clan? I really do have a whole clan of relatives here. And they really are my family. They love me and I love them. Suddenly, the thought from earlier about being alone seemed so ridiculous. Talitha was surrounded by more people - people who really cared, people who really mattered, people who were "real" people - than she had ever been in her entire life. These people truly were like her grandfather. They were exactly as God had created them and were beautiful in their own right, and proud of who and what they were.

"So sorry, Calvin," apologized Talitha. "I didn't realize I was so popular."

"It seems you've become the Queen of Cedar Mountain."

"No, I'm just like the rest of the people here. They're all,"

"I heard that," interrupted Calvin, speaking of the beep announcing another caller. "Why don't you go and be with your family? They've actually answered the question I called about in the first place. Seems like you're doing 'mighty fine,' as they say in the south."

A bright laugh came through the phone. "Yes, I am," she confessed with a bubbly smile. "And I don't think I realized how fine until this evening about eight o'clock."

"You take care, kid. Catch you later."

Talitha answered calls for nearly an hour before the phone went quiet. *Happy New Year, God.* She stared up at the beautiful moon, basking its light across the mountains, making the air whiter than it could ever have been from the light of bursting fireworks.

"Hah!" she laughed aloud. *Guess He can prove that He can put on the best fireworks show, too!*

At two in the morning, she put aside her novel and reached to turn out the bedside table lamp, perfect for reading. *Thank goodness, Flora liked to read in bed at night, too.* This one lamp had easily become her favorite thing in the house.

However, as she placed her hand on the pull switch, an urge to read her Bible struck her, as real as if someone's hand had tapped on her shoulder. She got up and looked in the bookcase for the Bible that had been presented to her in recognition of her high school graduation. It looked exactly as it had then, with all of the pages intact and the gold edging on the pages still glistening, from lack of use.

What would You like for me to read this evening? she smiled as she climbed back into the bed. Talitha closed her eyes, reached her fingers to a spot on the pages, feeling exactly as she had as a small child at the school carnival when she played her favorite game of "Go Fish," closing her eyes and swinging the string on the end of a fishing pole over a curtain where someone attached a prize – selected just for her – to the clothespin on the end of the line. Only now instead of a string on a fishing pole, she opened the pages of her Bible to reveal a special passage of scripture chosen just for her.

Mark 16:15, she read silently. "And he said to them, 'Go into all the world and proclaim the good news to the whole creation.'"

"Lord," came the audible words, "I'm not a minister. What can these words possibly have to do with me?"

She sat there for a few minutes, holding the Bible open and staring at the verse. *Fishing, huh? Can't I throw this verse in and go after another one?*

But Talitha knew the answer to that, for her grandfather had taught her that every verse in that massive book applied to her; that at any given time, the words she needed to hear were contained within those pages.

She took a huge breath and blew it out as she closed the Bible. Instead of putting the book back on the shelf where it had been, Talitha laid it on top of her novel on the bedside table and turned out the light.

It was indeed a Happy New Year.

Chapter 38

*N*ew *Year's Day! Time to get up. I don't want to waste one minute of today.*

Talitha quickly got dressed and turned on the laptop. While waiting for it to load, she opened all the shades in the house, catching a glimpse of last night's moon, still hanging on in its attempt to not let go of the prior year. She snickered. *Seems it knows what day it is, too.*

Unable to resist the urge to go outside and say, "Good morning!" to the world on the beginning of this new year, she hastened to the front yard and looked up at the sky already promising a perfect day. A beautiful clear blue, boasting of clean, fresh air, Talitha noticed that jet streams streaked across the sky, going in every direction. Considering that very few planes flew over her house, the wisps of white seemed a strange sight.

She took off around the house, running in every direction like the jet streams, with her arms outstretched and her head held back. Twirling in circles, she gave a small laugh. *I do hope that Burrell and Flora aren't up yet. They'll think I'm doing imitations of Maria from "Sound of Music" out here!*

Instantly, the irony of that thought struck her, for she was standing right between two mountains, with countless others visible in the distance, feeling like the hills truly *were* alive with "the sound of music."

"There's a certain music and charm to that place," Talitha remembered hearing from a customer in Kelly's on the day she'd first driven to Cedar Mountain and discovered her own music and charm in the air. *And seen the red door being painted on the church.*

Suddenly, she realized she'd just received her first blessing for the new year - the perception that she was not alone, nor would she ever be. For she was surrounded by her friends, her neighbors, her "brothers and sisters" - literally in every direction - she reasoned as she looked back up at the numerous jet streams.

The morning had made it quite evident that "He's got the whole world in His hands." *And me, too!*

Talitha hurried back into the cottage to begin another dream she'd had since her childhood, a dream she'd never shared with anyone, as she sat down at the laptop and typed the rough draft of a chapter for her first novel.

Chapter 39

The small cottage had been transformed into a writer's retreat. Hanging beside the front door, where once had hung a welcome sign, was a plaque that read, "Talitha's Writing Nest" and was decorated with petunias and hummingbirds – the same ones that matched the pillow cases and quilt rack in her bedroom. The furniture in the dining area had been replaced with desks, tables and drawers that held computers, printers and office supplies. File cabinets stood in the corners of the living room, filled bookshelves lined the walls; it looked like a set-up every newspaper reporter would die for.

Only a few pieces of "real" furniture remained in the living room, and a small table and chairs had been placed in the middle of the floor for those times when she felt the need for a formal meal. However, it was used mostly for a worktable as it had a glass top with a shelf underneath. She could place her notes on the shelf, her laptop on the glass, and sit in front of any window or door to see whatever mountain, creek or waterfall scene she wanted while typing away on whatever project was due at the time.

Flora had even redone the walls in black and antique white, with the help of Randy and Michael and all the folk who pitched in one Saturday to cover the walls on one side of the living room with sheets of old sheet music. Given her artistic talent, Randy's precision rock-laying skills, Michael's sense of humor and Uncle Burrell's ability to "fix anything," the wall was not only beautiful, but a myriad of intriguing personalities and musical inspiration.

And in front of the wall sat the old piano from Blue Ridge Baptist Church, which had been replaced by a hefty donation from an unknown individual – that only Talitha knew. On the top of it stood a small grapevine tree with one lone ornament hanging from it – a little girl holding a doll in one hand and seated at a piano, which she played with the other hand. Opposite the tree on the other side of the top was a framed picture - the Blue Ridge Baptist Church with its crimson red door and the sunset hitting the stained glass windows, just so, to make it appear that the church was full of life inside. But for Talitha, the focal point of the entire room was the music rack on the piano – where the hymnbook was turned to page 367 . . . *The Church in the Wildwood.*

The Church in the Wildwood

There's a church in the valley by the wildwood,
No lovelier spot in the dale;
No place is so dear to my childhood
As the little brown church in the dale.

CHORUS: Oh, come, come, come, come,
Come to the church in the wildwood,
Oh, come to the church in the vale.
No spot is so dear to my childhood
As the little brown church in the dale.

Oh, come to the church in the wildwood,
To the trees where the wild flowers bloom;
Where the parting hymn will be chanted,
We will weep by the side of the tomb. CHORUS

How sweet on a clear Sunday morning,
To list to the clear ringing bell;
Its tones so sweetly are calling,
Oh, come to the church in the vale. CHORUS

From the church in the valley by the wildwood,
When day fades away into night,
I would fain from this spot of my childhood
Wing my way to the mansions of light.

CHORUS: Oh, come, come, come, come,
Come to the church in the wildwood,
Oh, come to the church in the vale.
No spot is so dear to my childhood
As the little brown church in the dale.

William S. Pitts

CEDAR MOUNTAIN COOKIN'

Cedar Mountain is full of wonderful recipes. Recipes for
soap, recipes for uncomparable food - especially desserts - and
recipes for . . . well, there's some family secrets we just don't
talk about! But up on my side of the mountain, we all look
for the dishes of Mary Jane Howard at the church socials.
Here are a few of Mary Jane's favorite recipes. - - CR?

SNOWFLAKE COOKIES

1 lb. butter, softened
1 cup white sugar
3 cups all-purpose flour
1 tsp. vanilla
1 1/2 cups potato chips, crushed, but not too fine

Cream butter and sugar with a mixer. Add flour and vanilla. By hand, stir in crushed potato chips and mix gently. Drop on ungreased cookie sheet (a heaping teaspoon per cookie).

Bake at 325 degrees until slightly golden (aboutt 12-13 minutes). Sprinkle with powdered sugar.

PINE BARK

1 sticks butter (NO substitutes)
1 cup light brown sugar
1 12-oz. pkg. of chocolate morsels

Combine butter and sugar and boil for 3 minutes.

First, line a 10x15" jelly roll pan with aluminum foil. Spread a bottom layer with saltine crackers. Drizzle the crackers with the brown sugar mixture.

Bake at 325 degrees for 10 minutes. Sprinkle with a 12-oz. pkg. of chocolate morsels and spread when melted. Let cool and break into pieces.

POPPYSEED CHICKEN

2 lbs. chicken, cooked and deboned
1 can cream of chicken soup
1 8-oz. carton of sour cream
1 1/2 cups of Ritz Cracker crumbs
1 stick of melted butter
3 TBL. poppy seeds
Salt to taste

Mix butter, cracker crumbs and poppyseed. Layer 3/4 of mixture on bottom of 1 1/2 quart casserole dish. Reserve 1/4 for topping. Mix chicken, salt, soup and sour cream. Place on top of cracker crumbs. Top with remaining cracker crumbs.

Bake at 350 degrees for 30 minutes or until it bubbles. Serves 6.

CHICKEN SPECTACULAR

3 cups cooked chicken, coarsely chopped
1 pkg. Uncle Ben's Wild & White Rice, cooked in chicken broth
1 can cream of celery soup
1 medium jar of sliced pimentos, drained
1 medium onion, chopped
2 cans of French-style green beans, drained
1 cup mayonnaise
1 can of diced water chestnuts
Salt and pepper

Mix all ingredients. Bake at 350 degrees for 30 minutes.

Foreword to Questions & Reflections

Many people reach the mid point of their lives and then suddenly realize that they are not fulfilling their dream. It doesn't matter whether that dream has been alive since childhood or whether it is a newly desired goal. It is personal and it belongs to you, and if you are dwelling on it, you have obviously not fulfilled it.

There are many factors that force us to face our dreams and goals - some pleasant reminders, some terrifying realities - and those factors can come from a plethora of sources. Like Talitha in *Church in the Wildwood*, it is often an unplanned event that sparks us into taking an honest look at ourselves and what worthwhile things we have done with our lives.

It is my prayer that *Church in the Wildwood* will either be that spark for you, or serve to help you face the things in your life holding you back from reaching your life's goal or dream. More than that, I hope it challenged you to pray about whether your dream is YOUR dream or GOD'S dream for you.

May you be blessed with peace in living out your purposeful dream in life.

C. J. Didymus

Questions & Reflections

Whether you are reading these questions individually, or as part of a Bible study or reading group, you are encouraged to let the words and ideas flow freely as you reflect on your own life and situation. In fact, I recommend that you write your answers on a piece of paper and place them inside the back cover of this book. Come back to them - a day later, a week later, a month later, or even years laters. Whenever you come back, God's love and mercy will be the same. Remember, there is nothing too great to keep you from accepting and reaching God's dream for your life.

~ CR?

1) How often do you talk to God about your dream for your life?

2) Are you fulfilling what you feel is your ultimate goal, the one divinely chosen for you?

3)If not, what is standing in the way of you striving to reach that dream or goal?

4) What steps can you take to bring you closer to fulfilling that dream? And remember, faith *can* move a mountain!

4) Where do you go to spend time reflecting with God? Are you truly listening for the Almighty's voice to help you fulfil your dream?

Reality Fiction

The writing style of Catherine Ritch Guess has become synonymous with the term "Reality Fiction" since she opened her own niche in the inspirational market nearly three years ago.

Her novels, most of which are based in real settings, feature realistic characters and situations of contemporary society, and are spiced with historical facts. Although the stories, characters and locales are used fictitiously, her mission is that readers will find themselves within the pages of her writings.

From the letters she receives, it is obvious that her idea of Reality Fiction is working as it ministers to her readers. She intends her work to plant seeds and meet the needs of individuals who would never venture inside a house of worship or pick up a Bible. And for believers, she strives to help strengthen their spiritual lives by weaving a wealth of theology between the lines.

Her message is "if God can love the characters within my pages, He can love everyone." It is her hope and dream that readers will be uplifted in their own individual lives and situations through her characters and their stories.

UPCOMING RELEASES
of
CRM BOOKS

Musical Sculptures
Musical CD by Catherine Ritch Guess

Fall Fresh on Me
Musical CD by Angel Christ

Kipper Finds a Home: A White Squirrel Parable
by Catherine Ritch Guess

For the Beauty of the Earth
Catherine Ritch Guess

LIFE DRAWINGS: Beginnings, Plans and Dreams
Dave McCamon

Tis So Sweet
Catherine Ritch Guess

¡Ole! in a Manger
Jayne Jaudon Ferrer

The Midnight Clear
Catherine Ritch Guess

Broken Spirit
John Shivers

¡Ole! in a Manger
Jayne Jaudon Ferrer

You've read about the best Christmas pageant ever –
now read about the worst

Friendship Community Church is on its last legs. Attendance is down, giving is down, and the future does not look bright. When committee chair Myrna Malloy suggests doing a Christmas pageant to lift spirits, everyone thinks she's crazy. And maybe she is: between an attitudinal angel, a hormonal Wise Woman, "camels" gone berserk, and not a single contender for the role of Baby Jesus, this is shaping up to be a nativity nightmare. *¡Ole! in a Manger,* from author Jayne Jaudon Ferrer, features such chapters as "Rise Up Shepherds and Holler," "Deck the Halls with Cows, By Golly," "Lo, How Our Foes Are Looming," "Hark, the Imperiled Angels Sing," and "Whose Child Is This?!" Don't miss this hilarious, heartwarming story from CRM BOOKS.

Available October 1st, 2005

The Midnight Clear
Catherine Ritch Guess

With Guess' third volume of the Shooting Star Series, which fictionally features NASCAR great Dale Jarrett, parties are already being planned around the country for schools, churches, bookstores, and NASCAR fans - all in anticipation of the release of *The Midnight Clear*, which will be on November 4th - at MIDNIGHT, of course!

A book for every reader, the purchase of *The Midnight Clear* is a great way to give a Christmas gift that keeps on giving. A part of the proceeds from all four volumes of the Shooting Star Series is going to the Dale Jarrett Foundation and Give Kids the World Village and all sales on November 4th, 2005, will benefit the new children's hospital at NorthEast Medical Center in Concord, NC - the setting for the book.

PLANTING SEEDS . . .
SOWING YOUNG AUTHORS

One of the goals of CRM BOOKS is to inspire others, not only through the publication of uplifting books, but also by encouraging talented young people to pursue their art and their dreams. Catherine Ritch Guess, known for planting seeds wherever she goes, has agreed to join forces with CRM BOOKS' editors to begin an annual contest to identify young authors and illustrators.

Each year, a theme will be presented and, each year, CRM BOOKS will solicit entries from students around the country. The winning selections will be published in an annual anthology, with the Grand Prize winner receiving the opportunity to have Guess and another of our authors/artists visit his/her school for a special appearance and writing class.

For more information, visit www.ciridmus.com

About the Artist

RuthEllen Boerman discovered her God-given talent for painting in 1983, while helping her son with a school project. After appearing at art festivals and craft shows, and experiencing an emotionally trying time and "burn-out," she felt God was molding her to become a Christian artist.

With the success of her most popular print, *The True Vine*, RuthEllen was sure the Lord wanted her to devote the majority of her time to Christian art. Almost all of her paintings contain hidden religious objects or symbols, and most carry a spiritual message.

Boerman recently completed painting a series of twelve paintings based on the 23rd Psalm, and *True Vine II*. She also does commissioned works of homes and country scenes.

RuthEllen and her husband, Joe, were married in Marie's Chapel in Edneyville, North Carolina, which is the church used for the cover art of *Church in the Wildwood*. They live in Hendersonville, North Carolina.

About the Author

Catherine Ritch Guess, also a published composer, spent thirty-four years of her life as an Organist/Minister of Music before creating her niche in the world of inspirational literature.

Guess, who holds degrees in Church Music, Music Education and a Master's Degree in Christian Education, is a Diaconal Minister of the United Methodist Church. She is currently appointed as the Circuit Riding Musician, a position which allows her to serve globally through her writing, speaking and musical talents.

A native of North Carolina, Catherine resides in Cedar Mountain where she is busy completing *The Midnight Clear*, the third book of her Shooting Star Series (which features NASCAR great Dale Jarrett) and her third Sandman Series novel, *Victory in Jesus*. Between recording two new CDs of her musical arrangements, she is getting ready for the release of two other novels, *For the Beauty of the Earth* and *'Tis So Sweet*.